What people are s

The Pac-Man F

Alex Wade has written a rattling good book, as ravenous and riveting as his main character, Pac-Man, whose adventures take us from the frictionless glide through the shopping centre to the dank corners of the postmodern neo-liberal world and our many forms of resistance against it, whether in a Balkan minefield or a cannabis factory. On the way Alex Wade weaves a tantalizing guide through the labyrinths of contemporary capitalism. Read it and be shocked into seeing both the real and the hyperreal in unexpected ways. Better still, read it twice; it's short and lively. Like playing Pac-Man, it's addictive.

Dennis Smith, Emeritus Professor of Sociology, Loughborough University

Pac-Man can be regarded as the convenient poster child of video game culture. It came from a desire to explore non-violence in game design when the popularity of space shooters was reaching its apex, and years before Mike Edwards' *Realm of Impossibilities* or Richard Garriott's *Ultima IV* adopted a similar design motto. It was built around the universally desirable theme of eating and is still lauded as an attempt to attract a wider demographic, including women. That story has already been told. Alex Wade doesn't simply revisit this landmark moment in game history. Moving away from a cute-ified glorification of an important figure, his account explores the darker half of this poster child. It dives into the open mouth to explore the underbelly of the yellow munching beast: capitalism.

From the smooth consumption occurring in its labyrinths to the constant surveillance of algorithms lurking beneath the googly eyes of ghosts, and the sad inevitability of terror attacks

– or a kill screen – in these homogenised worlds made for a consumer-tourist always on the move, Pac-Man resonates with the current neoliberal condition. In a constantly accelerated conflict, power pellets provide some welfare and a momentary reversal of fortune. This powerful formula has grown into one of the most essential forms of reinforcement, forging our consumption of video games, our technological and even social habitus. Pac-Man as a symbol of the world? Wade allows us to connect the dots.

Carl Therrien, Adjunct Professor, University of Montreal

Wade expertly pulls apart one of video gaming's most iconic titles to discover layer upon layer of meaning, drawing comparisons between Namco's globally-recognised pill-gobbler and the often shadowy worlds of capitalism, politics and much more besides, making it abundantly clear that there's much more to these pixellated classics of yesteryear than meets the eye.

Damien McFerran, Editor, *Nintendo Life* and Gaming and Tech Journalist

The *Pac-Man* Principle

A User's Guide to Capitalism

The *Pac-Man* Principle

A User's Guide to Capitalism

Alex Wade

Winchester, UK
Washington, USA

First published by Zero Books, 2018
Zero Books is an imprint of John Hunt Publishing Ltd., No. 3 East St., Alresford,
Hampshire SO24 9EE, UK
office1@jhpbooks.net
www.johnhuntpublishing.com
www.zero-books.net

For distributor details and how to order please visit the 'Ordering' section on our website.

Text copyright: Alex Wade 2017

ISBN: 978 1 78535 605 6
978 1 78535 606 3 (ebook)
Library of Congress Control Number: 2017938669

A CIP catalogue record for this book is available from the British Library.

Design: Stuart Davies

Printed and bound by CPI Group (UK) Ltd, Croydon, CR0 4YY, UK

We operate a distinctive and ethical publishing philosophy in
all areas of our business, from our global network of authors to
production and worldwide distribution.

Contents

For Ania, my original power-pill.

Alex Wade is a sociologist based in the Faculty of Health, Education and Life Sciences at Birmingham City University, UK. He has written previously on simulations, space and time and French social theory. He is currently engaged in excavating the history of videogames and a book examining the many histories of videogames in the UK, *Playback: A Genealogy of 1980s British Videogames*, was published in 2016. *The Pac-Man Principle* is his second book. He lives in Leicestershire with his wife and two daughters. He can be contacted at alex.wade@bcu.ac.uk.

1

In Defence of *Pac-Man*

The eponymous arcade game, featuring the pill-popping, yellow pie chart, Pac-Man, was developed by Toru Iwatani and published by Namco in 1980. The ghost-chasing fruitarian is nearly forty years old. As he approaches the abyss of middle age, his prolific output shows no sign of slowing. Namco's release of *Pac-Man 256*, in 2015, means that in the 35 years since his inception, Pac-Man had appeared in over 50 individual videogames across practically every platform ever released. With videogames' position as the pre-eminent media form of the 21st century, Pac-Man's ubiquity and prestige in popular media is assured. Debuts in Saturday morning kids cartoon shows, pinball tables, music singles, card-games, and, long before *Pokémon Go*, augmented reality games, mean that the social and cultural influence reaches far beyond the dark, dank realms of the arcade and the games room. Filipino boxer Manny Pacquiao adopted 'Pac-Man' as his ring name during his run towards being one of the greatest boxers to have ever lived; a nebula of the Cassiopeia constellation was attributed with his moniker as the collection of stars resembles Pac-Man chomping down on a power pill; the 'Pac-Man defence' is a business strategy employed by corporations which reverses a hostile takeover by buying shares in the aggressor corporation, whilst Norwegian scientists are using a miniaturised version of Pac-Man's maze to investigate the interaction of microorganisms. This legion of examples demonstrates how Pac-Man has come to be deified as one of the few videogame characters to truly attain what Henry Jenkins calls 'transmediality',[1] where cultural artefacts are deployed and utilised far outside of their host medium.

The Pac-Man defence is instructive of the true transmediality of the Pac-Man. The action of turning back on one's aggressor, as Pac-Man does with his ghostly pursuers, has infused the dominant economic, political, social and cultural model of the West: capitalism. As countless political economists have identified, the purest form of capitalism is predicated on the principle of the state of nature, that is, the survival of the fittest. Fortunately, as this book highlights, capitalism, for a variety of reasons, is rarely seen in these unbridled forms, but the Pac-Man defence is this idea very much at work. In the playground the bullied turns back upon the bully; in the workplace the worker stands up to the manager; in the wild the prey bears its claws to the predator. Before reaching this point though, the individual pupil, worker or animal must be coaxed and educated that this course of action, where the aggressor is automatically conferred with rights far beyond its ken, is inappropriate and unacceptable. In many societies this is an action conferred by a safety net which takes the form of welfare, education and health support: it is the check and balance to the state of nature. This is also undertaken by parents or carers, siblings or partners who will nurture the individual to react and push back against prevailing forces.

It is perhaps telling that Pac-Man himself was created as a prelapsarian character, reliant on the player for input, coaxing and nurturing. Pac-Man himself is helpless without a player guiding him around the maze: upon starting a game, with no player input, Pac-Man will start moving autonomously before headbanging the wall of the maze. This mindless wandering is manifest in the physiological characteristics of Pac-Man. In classic iterations such as *Pac-Man Championship Edition*, Pac-Man has no eyes and relies entirely on the player for guidance and safety in the smooth spaces garnered by the relatively hostile environment of the classical labyrinth. It is interesting then, that even in the now legendary and widely-cited interview with Susan Lammers, Iwatani's perception of Pac-Man as an innocent caught in this state of nature is so often overlooked, seeing his character as one who 'hasn't been educated to discern between good and evil. He acts more like a small child than a grown-up person. Think of him as a child learning in the course of his daily activities'.[2] Pac-Man as a character, alone in a maze, is amazed at this isolation, so resorts to one of the universals of human existence, eating, in order to survive. For modern societies, need has been supplanted by greed as the public flaunting of eating as a status symbol is rivalled only by the pornographic sheen of advertising that accompanies it. Viewed in this way it is possible to see how Pac-Man becomes a poster child for capitalism, as Iwatani continues, he's 'indiscriminate because he's naive. But he learns from experience'.[3] Therefore, the ideal consumer, formed of universal need in the crucible of a labyrinth, becomes the ideal learner-worker to be deployed within the state of nature of capitalism, who will turn back on his aggressors when given the opportunity.

Indeed, Iwatani continues on to say that the inspiration for Pac-Man arises primarily from consumption. Eating food is a universal for living things and a videogame which focussed on this would have equal universal appeal to young and old, male and female, irrespective of race, nation and class. The use of the Japanese symbol kuchi 口 was the initial inspiration, which connotes with 'hole' or 'opening', usually to a body. As Iwatani identifies, the manipulation of symbols has a specific and special power within language, so that the universality of kuchi extends to mastication, digestion, defecation and even sex. Meaning is not conferred, but is, like Kuchi (pun intended), particularly open to interpretation, as the term has been adopted and adapted into American English with the term 'coochi', a vulgar expression for female genitalia, presumably a linguistic by-product of the American occupation of Japan following World War II. The importance of the opening to Pac-Man's origin story extends as far to the – partly upheld – belief that the final shape of Pac-Man himself arose from Iwatani spying a pizza with a slice taken out of it.

As Toru Iwatani's afterword to this book outlines *Pac-Man* is a game about bridging the differences that existed in arcade game play at the time. Where many games focussed on shooting (e.g. *Space Invaders*), *Pac-Man* concentrated on universals of existence. If the human race proves anything it is that even in (or especially in) universality there is diversity and difference. *Pac-Man* addressed this contradiction, and in many ways is symbolic of the postmodern condition. In its flexibility and inclusiveness it uses the touchstones of postmodernism. The equity of 'high' and 'low' culture, textual wordplay, the increasing importance of games and access to information as a post-industrial society, in thrall to the individual, looked to overcome traditional obstacles where not all people are equal. In an unbridled state of nature this would be seen as equality of opportunity as there is – theoretical – universal access to resources. In societies where safety nets and interventions exist, this may include racial, sexual and disability equality enshrined in legislation which attempts to provide some semblance of equity through taxation and redistribution.

Thoughtfully and gracefully, and in keeping with the postmodern moment, Iwatani aimed to create a videogame where the traditional distinctions between work and play, private and public, black and white, male and female, did not apply. As discussed below, videogames, as part of a long and rich tradition of games, are unquestionably tied to a learning experience. Amusement arcades, where the most technologically advanced arcade games were located, were seen as a transitional space between the public and the private, and unlike bars and pubs, were not subject to laws limiting access to under-18s. People went to play games and they appealed to all. This is breathlessly documented in Martin Amis's visual extravaganza *Invasion of the Space Invaders*, where he witnesses an actress whose case of 'Pac-Man hand' was so severe that it resembled blood pudding.[4]

4

Still, as a developer working for a corporation whose main aim is to make money, the pursuit of equality through the pleasure principle of consumption is also good for profits.

Similarly, postmodernism through legislation or positive action looks to overcome inequalities, for better or for worse, but always in the pursuit of profit. For instance, women of the mid and late 20th century were impelled to go out to work. This is, in many cases, seen as liberation and emancipation, with the struggle for equality of pay and opportunity continuing to this day. Less widely discussed are some of the effects of this. In spite of a litany of extra people being in work, living standards have stagnated and in many countries have fallen: everyone is working more for less. Women undertake the 'triple shift' of care for young and old relatives whilst working full-time: in the quest for having it all, there is nothing left. The emotional labour of caring for children and elderly relatives has been partially contracted out to nurseries and care homes which is, usually, undertaken by women, often immigrants, who work with soul-destroying monotony cleaning *kuchi* and its variant excretions. While it remains questionable if this care can be outsourced offshore, many of these nurturing tasks still need to be done in the domestic environment, as chapter four shows, so as to prepare for, or repair for, the state of nature which is sold to us and masquerades as 'freedom'. Freedom to choose, freedom to vote, interest-free credit cards, free labour (internships), free-trade zones, free from Europe, free-fire zone, nuclear-free, free-data, free-Internet. It is not the lack of freedom, but a surfeit of it which is the cause of concern of those parents, teachers, social workers, youth leaders, nurses, midwives, charged with bringing young, naive beings into the world so that they can be guided and coaxed to live, thrive and survive in smooth, cool, postmodern spaces.

Play and games have always been attributed with the predicate of learning. Apart from the classic texts by Johan

Huizinga and Roger Caillois, Freud used the interaction between child and parent as a means to treat through psychoanalysis and there is a burgeoning of literature and enterprise around simulations, serious games and gamification, where, in truly flexible and postmodern fashion, the boundaries between work and play, toil and leisure are liquidised (exams can be fun too) and imbibed as human factors, skills which are important to the dominant economic model seen in areas as diverse and universal as decision-making, communication, teamwork and leadership. Using play and games as means to an end, and not as the young, naive child does, merely as an ends within itself, is innovative and creative. Medical simulations permit students to learn and make mistakes in an anodyne environment, whilst trainee pilots can gain operational hours in a passenger jet without putting 200 people at risk when buying the farm.

It is unsurprising that Iwatani was also an advocate of this philosophy, as long as it chimed with the corporation's pursuit of profit: 'I think that unless education is fun and entertaining, people won't learn... there are many people with enough interest to pay good money for educational software'.[5] Games that provide something beyond their own context mesh coherently with the concept of transmediality and fit with the professed aims of capitalism to exploit any and all milieu, including personal interests, in the ephemeral search for profit.[6] Proof of this is seen in the ways in which videogame players sign up to a free beta test and effectively crash test the – usually flawed – software to destruction. This is a labour-intensive process which may have been previously undertaken by play-testers hoping for a break in the videogames industry but by being marketed as having 'early access' to a desirable piece of software, much of this labour can be virtually and willingly outsourced, all in the name of freedom: freedom from cost to the corporation and freedom to attain early access to desirable software. This example merely endorses the line of thinking that innovation is impossible without having some competitive element in the economic process. Games then have a double role to play here in terms of engendering competition between individuals (capitalism) with pre-agreed rules and outcomes, and also providing the basis for cooperation (checks and balances) to achieve the best outcome for all.

Pac-Man is a good early example from a videogame of seeing this in action. Pac-Man is that naive, innocent child, who would like to consume for pleasure and turn the table on the bully ghosts, but can only do this with intervention and guidance from another whose motivation is to eat as many ghosts, fruit, dots and pills as possible so that they can enter their three letter initials on the high score table and attain kudos and public fame. Yet as Carly Kocurek highlights in an excellent essay about the influence of early coin-operated arcade games, it is not only the content of games which are directly linked to capitalism, but also the practices that are undertaken around them, in their usage and their play. With the child playing with a tea set, there is an open-endedness conferred on whether she serves her dolls high tea, or in a pique of creative destruction, decides to smash the cups against the wall. For those playing an arcade game, the rules are very much set and there is little scope for innovation in the *practice* of play, no matter how much innovation is employed in the design and development of the game. This is because early arcade games, partly due to technical limitations, but mainly due to increasing revenue streams, were often based on the twin tenets of being extremely difficult, which meant a great deal of expenditure to attain proficiency, but were also closely tied to progression i.e. moving from one level to the next in pursuit of the high score, rather than emergence where more of the game is revealed the longer it is played.

For the pay-to-play model common to arcade games to be proficient it was necessary to become highly skilled at following the rules laid down in and by the game. This is why, as chapter six explains, guidebooks educating players in how to 'game' or 'play' the system proved to be so popular. To play well, to follow the rules and the objectives laid down by the game meant that the 'longer a player can play, the more points he can earn, and the more clout he has in the competitive social environment of the arcade'.[7] It is not possible for instance, as Martin Amis dreams of doing, of sending Pac-Man into the ghosts' den at the centre of the screen: to do so would lead to certain dematerialisation of Pac-Man. It does, however, mean that if the game is played at a high level for a long period of time, it would be possible to stretch out the 10p put into the machine for hours, fulfilling the protestant work ethic identified by Max Weber where less is indubitably more.

Yet, again, as with all elements of capitalism there are contradictions and, in this instance, the conceit of less is more has an inverse legacy, the results of which are still being revealed today. The arcade and the games within it are a playful, postmodern spin on the state of nature. They are the embodiment of what philosopher David Harvey calls 'flexible accumulation'[8] where new spaces are opened to capitalism and the processes common to capitalism are intensified. One credit can be stretched to last all day; hard work is rewarded by extended play. For the children who grew up in the arcade of the 1980s, this is normal and normed behaviour. For the late 1990s meritocracies of Europe and America where these children became adults, the pay-to-play economic model was adopted wholesale: a necessary bargain of citizenship was that rights and responsibilities were in check and balance: if you had no job, you had to work at getting one; you have a right to smoke, but a responsibility not to in public. The contemporary flexibility in work, such as freelancing, zero hours and fixed term contracts are pay-to-play models shifted from consumption to labour. The high scores that were accumulated were not rewarded by extra lives or names as three letter initials, but credit cards,

125% mortgages and payday loans validated by the names of signatures on loan forms, that ultimately in 2008 meant that even the banks couldn't afford to pay to play anymore, the tab for which governments are still picking up: cheques and balances indeed.

The question raised is: how to protect ourselves from a world where the sureties of the 'job for life' of industrial capitalism and the financial securities this offers have been replaced by the flexible and ephemeral accumulation of tweets, high scores and Facebook friends and five-digit credit card statements? It is tempting to look towards old institutions such as the National Health Service for solace. Like, or perhaps more than capitalism itself, though, the NHS, with its position as a secular religion in the UK, is in crisis. Partly, this is due to it running unmanageable and unserviceable levels of debt as New Labour inflicted capital as contagion in the form of off-book Private Finance Initiatives. The net gain was shiny new hospitals and innovative heart surgery techniques, but the cost was the replacement of healthcare staff with metrics and lives with deaths. Yet, the aim of the NHS has always been one of prevention rather than cure. It is, after all, more cost-effective to provide a teenager with a condom and a perfunctory didactic lecture than pay £5000 for delivery and support of baby and family nine months later.

This is the concept of prophylaxis, where it is better to stop an occurrence than dealing with it later. It is a principle which is applied as equally to the administration of the state of war as the welfare state: the accretion of strategic nuclear weapons during the Cold War was founded on the idea of deterrence where only a president or first secretary with an interest in MAD (Mutually Assured Destruction) would dare to press the red button consigning the globe to nuclear desolation. What is fascinating for nuclear strategists is again the paradox that lies at the heart of their construction: it is not that they are suitable, for use, but that they are completely unsuitable, and in the hands of a rational actor (a president?) they will not be used. These are themes that are also common to videogames, particularly the genre of 'survival horror', where individuals are provided with unsuitable weapons and limited resources in unforgiving environments whilst trying to surmount murderous odds. Electronic Arts' *Dead Space* is an excellent example of this: an engineer trapped on a failing starship fights hostile aliens with little more than a plasma cutter and audio recordings of lost shipmates, whilst Frank West in *Dead Rising* has a welter of weapons at his disposal to fight zombies in a shopping mall, but none are more intentionally ludicrous than swinging a mannequin or popping a tennis ball gun at the undead menace.

In and of themselves, these are weapons of prophylaxis. Unsuited to the task, they act more as a defence, or deterrence, against attack than first strike weapons which are used as a means of attack in shooting games from *Combat* to *Call of Duty*. *Pac-Man*, as the first game to feature the now common 'power-up', where a character is augmented and assumes special capabilities, was also the first game to use prophylaxis as a weapon. As Martin Amis observes the power pills which allow Pac-Man to undertake the Pac-Man Defence and turn back against the aggressor are a 'legitimate defensive tool – good for tight corners as well as accumulating points'.[9] This places *Pac-Man* at the genealogical head of survival games, where as we have already seen, environments and enemies propel Pac-Man into a state of nature which his naiveté ill-prepares him for, but seeks to learn about rapidly. There is no doubt that this is a game of survival; it is quite literally a matter of being quick or being dead.

The intersection between a permanent state of war, which encompassed the whole globe, but in a typical nuclear paradox kept the warring parties from firing direct shots at one another, and the welfare state, which aims to protect civilians by giving shots to people, and in a medical paradox, take the form of the disease themselves, in the form of vaccination, demonstrates the precarious twin bind on which capitalism teeters. It is at once responsible for ensuring that the bottom line is cut to an edge whereby it continually quivers on the precipice of its own suicide and self-destruction. There is also a general awareness in the governments of the world that a healthy workforce is a productive workforce and that it can be put to work by capital in its quest for profit. Life-expectancy, infant mortality, morbidity indexes are indicators which lie at the heart of good capitalist societies. Similarly, the war machine which powers so much investment and expenditure, employment and taxation provides a safe, prophylactic environment for the system to operate within.

As this chapter has shown, the contradictions and twin binds of capitalism are manifested across a range of social and cultural milieu, many of which we interact with on a daily basis. From the opening of the mouth to the hole of the rectum, rights and responsibilities, checks and balances, the welfare state to the warfare state, predators to prey, education to nuclear strategy, they are experiences that are as common to Pac-Man the character as to the player of the game. The state-of-nature of unbridled capitalism, which dispassionately and amorally attempts to infuse all areas of daily life, is resisted at an elemental and very human level by the concept of prophylaxis. Whether this takes the form of a pill or a weapon, or, in Pac-Man's case the pill *as* a weapon, they both act as the same manner on the system which pays host to it, which gives it substance and meaning. As Jean Baudrillard notes when 'a certain saturation point is reached, such systems effect this reversal and undergo this alteration willy-nilly and thus tend to self destruct'.[10] This gives credence to the ongoing perception of capitalism lurching from one crisis to another, without ever actually self-destructing: it is held in place by checks and balances of systems which at once prevent the descent into an unbridled state of nature, but at the same time prevent the hegemony of a command economy or police state.

The problem with much critical theory is that it doesn't offer an escape route, or a way out. Baudrillard twists this problem inside out and states that the answers come from within the system: like playing a game of Whack-a-Mole, or waging preventative, prophylactic wars against despotic leaders in the Middle East, the harder and quicker we try to eradicate the enemy the harder it becomes to control the outcome. For this reason, the proponent of the Pac-Man Principle must examine the system that gives rise to it to find the answers that lie within. Firstly, this means examining the spaces and times constructed and inhabited by Pac-Man and whether these classical labyrinths and modern mazes offer ingress and egress, and indeed, where they will lead us to.

2

Speed and Space: The Places and Times of *Pac-Man*

If the entrances and exits to a capitalist system are so in thrall to its own demise, then they are equally held in place by the checks and balances of built-in prophylaxis. This chapter explores these contradictory times and spaces through the environments that Pac-Man inhabits. Alongside the classical labyrinths and the zero-sum game that a race against a timer, or the wall of the infamous 'killscreen' that Level 256 signifies (see chapter six), these are spaces and times that have significance for the player, the dot-munching avatar and the wider dominant social and cultural model found in the flexible accumulation common to postmodern capitalism. This at once gives rise to games such as *Pac-Man* and also allows us to operate with some semblance of competence within a world that sometimes feels a little like the recurring labyrinth which Pac-Man finds himself in: one that is bland, repetitive and difficult to escape from.

If this sounds like a Saturday brunch-time trip to a shopping centre, then this is perhaps not coincidental: the hollowed out, postmodern spaces, which enable frictionless, contactless, conspicuous consumption to take place, are, as we will see later, certainly in evidence in *Pac-Man*. Before considering the metaphorical space, the position of the game, both in its visual presentation and its orientation in everyday spaces, reveals much about *Pac-Man* and its importance to contemporary capitalist societies.

The transportability of arcade machines, which could be wedged into any corner which possessed a mains power outlet, enables *Pac-Man* to share in a rich genealogy of games that are able to be played and positioned in different environments.[1]

Each level on *Pac-Man* is referred to as a 'board' (a term it also shares with the 'board' on which the code is programmed) and has commonalities with 'board' games such as chess, pinball and bar skittles. Like these games, *Pac-Man* could be found in a welter of everyday spaces including newsagents, supermarkets, takeaways and laundromats. These are – conveniently – also arenas which are, unusually for Western culture, both cash rich *and* time rich. Individuals in these spaces would generally be mooching, 'killing time' waiting for and imbibing food, people, drink, laundry.

Their location in everyday spaces would also mean they captured a wide demographic. Passing trade would appeal as much to the schoolchild with pocket money as the tardy businessman buying guilt gifts for his wife on the way home from an overseas trip as the young mother whiling away a couple of moments whilst a toddler napped in their pushchair. The universality of appeal was reinforced by *Pac-Man* using only one joystick as an input method, in distinction to games such as *Asteroids* and *Defender* which had several buttons to control the ship and subsequent shooting. The orientation of coin-operated games and particularly *Pac-Man* in everyday spaces meant that they shared similar attributes to television, which, as Anna McCarthy has identified, has become 'ambient'[2] as it takes up residence in doctor's surgeries, on buses and in bars, achieving ubiquity to the point where it disappears from view.

Yet this positioning does not solely account for *Pac-Man*'s success. Its installation in these spaces is contingent on its own use of space within the game. Most obviously, and most tellingly, the plane, top-down, perspective of the maze permits the player to see the entirety of the game at any one time. Once again we can see the commonalities it has with other games which are set on a board such as chess, bar skittles and pinball. These are what I call 'tactically pure' games and do not hide information from the player. This is in distinction to emergent games, which include the majority of contemporary top-tier videogames, which are articulated along lines of complexity and hidden information. In some cases – such as the community chest in *Monopoly* and children's card games such as *Snap!* and *Dobble* – these games rely partly or wholly on the luck of the draw, or what the French sociologist Roger Caillois calls *alea*. *Pac-Man*, like chess, is a game reliant almost entirely on player skill and execution of that skill in competition, a component which Caillois terms *agon*.

In the realm of Pac-Land, it is interesting to note that the top-down perspective plays a significant part in the construction and comprehension of the game. *Pac-Man* defers to a classical structure which is similar to a maze or a labyrinth. Whilst the plane view was employed by *Pac-Man* because of technical limitations, this had the effect of freeing up the game to be tactically pure. For example, when you are in a maze and trying to find the way to the centre, there is a limited amount of skill involved. It is more likely that a process of trial and error is employed which draws considerably on luck or *alea*. The top-down approach removes this and defers to skill or *agon* as there is nothing hiding around a corner that cannot already be seen.

This removes much of the frustration as failure can only be attributed to a lack of skill in the player, not a deficiency in the design of the game. Yet, in an ongoing lesson to game-developers everywhere, the execution of the design remains as important as the production of the space. Another 1980 Namco maze chase game, *Rally-X*, was seen as the better fiscal prospect by Namco management. Its scrolling playfield and vibrant colours were seen as the state-of-the-art in arcade manufacture. However, the speed of the enemies in the initial levels was quicker than the player's avatar and the lack of tactical purity meant that it was too difficult to learn the patterns and fundamentals of the game when enemies appeared to have an inherent advantage, a predicate which reduced its wider popularity.

As the opening chapter discusses, one of Toru Iwatani's

professed aims with *Pac-Man* was to create a game that appealed in equal measure to women as well as men. This extends to the visual form of the game, which in its grid-like patterns are evocative of the mazes of early-modern England and ancient Greece. The role of the female, obviated in *Pac-Man* (at least until the release of *Ms. Pac-Man* a year later), is essential to the quest for success in pre-modern mazes. For example, in Greek legend, when faced with something akin to a mutation of the state-of-nature, Ariadne weaponises Theseus with a sword to kill the bull-man Minotaur at the sickened heart of the Athens labyrinth. More importantly, Ariadne's logistics chain extends to providing Theseus with a ball of thread to find his way out safely following the slaying. She provides a literal and literary escape route from the unicursality of the maze and the monomania of the monster. Later, in early modern England, mazes provided a 'safe place' similar to those proffered by simulations to students in the contemporary world. The maze meant that a woman could engage in a chase with a man and 'hold court', with some semblance of equity and equality, with no negative effect on her reputation or status. The use of a 'court' in a variety of games, particularly those with links to the aristocracy, such as real tennis, is another testament to this position as a safe place where machinations outside of everyday life can be experimented with. However, as the court of law accedes, rules still apply.

The 240 dots that Pac-Man must munch across the grid, interspersed with the four treats of power pills, mesh with modern fairy tales where there is necessity to escape back to safe places with lives intact. Like Ariadne's ball of thread, breadcrumbs are used by Gretel in the fairy tale *Hansel and Gretel* to guide the brother and sister to safety. The eating of the breadcrumbs by other animals demonstrates the difficulty of staying safe in a literal and literary state-of-nature and the futility of escaping away from the evil that resides at the dark heart of the labyrinth. This is perhaps a warning that is worth heeding twice over, the colourful, sugar-coated paraphernalia of fruit and bells that Pac-Man chomps on are reminiscent of the symbols of gambling with pure *alea* on fruit machines. Experimentation, which is common to the safe places of games, can, in itself, border on the gamble of stepping outside of the normal boundaries of everyday life and into the maze which permeates these narratives and structures of games. Identifying with this, Amis attributes *Pac-Man* with a 'childish whimsicality'.[3] Adroitness of thought, feminine maturity and childlike inventiveness can vanquish the ghosts and monsters of bedtime stories. Tucked up in bed, listening to the story of loss in *Hansel and Gretel*, the place where we feel safest is also the arena where we look to challenge the boundaries of that safety. Invariably (but not always), there is a happy ending which is akin to the survival horror experience of Pac-Man operating in the face of insurmountable odds, limited resources and hostile environments.

Unlike many of the debates that continue around the study of games of being either rule-based systems that sit separate from other media (ludology), or that games are a vehicle for telling stories (narratology), *Pac-Man* demands interpretation through its relationship to the past, present and futures of the labyrinth: this can take the form of the spaces of the labyrinth and the stories that are contained within them. This is a notion common to the position of labyrinths and their content, as Jorge Luis Borges observed in the mid-20th century, long before the inception of *Pac-Man*, 'everyone imagined two works, to no-one did it occur that the book and the maze were the same thing'.[4] Both the game's form, found in its one-joystick input mechanism, ease of rule-sets and tactical purity suggest a straightforward way *into* the game for the player, then the content, that is the story that it tells, suggests that there is an equally happy ending on the way *out* of the labyrinth and the maze. These are anodyne spaces that can be experimented with, but where nurture and culture should, all things being equal, overcome nature and science. Nevertheless, they remain, for the player of *Pac-Man* and Pac-Man himself, opposite sides of the same coin, there is danger, experimentation, ease of ingress and a happy egress. In this respect it engenders a similar position that Western individuals found themselves in during Cold War capitalism. It was not only the rise of flexible accumulation and microprocessor technologies, or even science and rationality which was vital to the West, but the *spirit* of capitalist democracies that were viewed as (rightly or wrongly) decidedly morally and ethically superior to the centralised command and control of eastern European economies.

The maze of rationality generated by mutually assured destruction and deterrence was balanced by the protection offered by weapons of prophylaxis: the Minotaur of Communism was held in check by spending on the warfare state. This thread was weaved into a safety net, in the shape of welfare structures which provided means of protection to their own populace against the more quotidian threats of disease and destitution. It is interesting that in this – relatively – safe place, protected from the mortal threats of war, narratives are weaved which imagine our own destruction. Borges envisages the Minotaur roaming the streets of Athens in *The House of Asterion*; post-Apocalyptic narratives from *Threads* to *The Stand* prevail at the *fin de siècle*. Many of the same silicon technologies which act as a prophylaxis and enable a utopia to be achieved simulate and anticipate the cessation of the West's safe place/state of nature duplicity. Like Pac-Man caught by a ghost and disappearing into the ether, we are at the end of history and, to the last man, obsessed by our own disappearance.

Whilst the space Pac-Man occupies is clearly classical in its topological structure and narrative content, there is an equal and parallel orientation towards hypermodernity. Frictionless and contactless, the smooth spaces that allow Pac-Man to move around the labyrinth away from the monsters and spectres bear obvious similarities to the spaces of consumption presented by postmodern capitalism. This is true of the position of the arcade cabinet in the locations of consumption outlined above, but also in areas which historically or contemporaneously mirror the darkened, subterranean spaces of the arcade. Always slightly surreptitious, arcades are places where, as the great videogame designer Al Alcorn observes, 'naughty things might happen'.[5] In this respect they draw upon and mirror other literal and metaphorical darkened underground spaces which provide the possibility for naughtiness, such as the speakeasy and snooker hall, strip club and strip mall.

Often these places require a special language, a code, to enter. The amusement arcade is no different, with the braggadocio of the three letter abbreviations of the high score table linked to the bravado of the extra life, the insertion and elongation of credit slid into a coin-slot viewed as the token of success, rather than how quickly credit can be spent; the power-up and smart bomb used equally as methods of defence and attack, prevention and cure.

There are also the more evident links of the game itself to the smooth spaces of consumption, the happy, mapped-out, shopping centre with its wide concourses and ease of arrival and departure in the car park and on the tram system. Whilst the shopping centre, unlike the dinginess of the classical labyrinth, is brashly-lit and its signposts provide ease of traversal, the obviation of any natural light, or even reference to the passage of time, places the individual in something which is akin to Pac-Man on a power pill, temporarily and irrepressibly able to munch through goods and crunch through credit with the end, both in egress and ingress, hidden from the consumer's view. The comedown can be hard to face. Like a visit to a TK Maxx, the shopping centre is easy to get into, but hard to leave, the satisfaction of shopping almost always accompanied by a slight niggle that, like the classical labyrinth itself, there is something mortal left in the centre of consumption when the red thread of money, or of blood, runs dry.

Commuting the largest possible transactions with the minimum amount of interaction is an inertia demanded by capitalism. In contrast to Baudrillard's own work in *The Consumer Society*, where human relationships and emotional labour are consumed as part of the transaction where the prettified smiles and idealised poses are key to the whole experience, contemporary transactions remove important elements of the human. Self-serve points, contactless payments, app-based fast-food ordering and swipe-screens in McDonald's actively remove human interaction from consumption. What perhaps would have made one purchase different to the next would have been the repartee, flirtation and perhaps even seduction associated with 'going shopping', the symbolic possibility, no matter how remote, of something naughty or dangerous happening, even in these safe, sanitised spaces.

Although not completely divorced from these relationships, the solitariness of Pac-Men wandering – and wondering – around a mall or a high street is really only punctuated by being pursued by ghosts. Individuals in superhero costumes impel us to buy pizza (through an app, of course) and the rejected, resigned eyes of chuggers who know that you're going to say no before they know they're going to talk to you. Shopping centres and arcades share some of the dichotomies at the heart of capitalism. They are simultaneously positioned as both public and private, accessible to all. Whilst in this space, there is an accent on permissiveness combined with prohibition. Demonstrations of 'individualism', bright hair, bright clothes, bright smiles are permitted, but demonstrations of dissatisfaction, of disagreement, are not only discouraged, but as a place where the public are permitted ingress by dint of the management company of Westfield, Hammerson or Prudential, are prohibited and illegal. These smooth spaces of capitalism, temporally sanitised and spatially manicured to within an inch of their life, do not allow the 'other' to be present unless there is a marked benefit to the contactless, cool consumerism where human relationships are no longer laboured, but detached and divorced from the other, from the human. In this state of nature, it is the solitary shopper, swiftly moving through space and screens, who is king.

The commonalities that the solitary shopper experiences are really only unified through the speed of transaction, clearly and sadly embodied in the human want to accumulate and the human need to pay for it. Speed in traversal and transaction is of the essence here. Being able to survive the murderous odds of the games and narratives of labyrinths, Ariadne's thread and Gretel's breadcrumbs demonstrate that speed of thought is the essence of survival to prevent being sucked into Borges' tale of Asterion whose melancholic minotaur shows the solitary sorrow of everyday life. *Pac-Man* conceives and applies speed as one of its central components. In its classical iterations, Pac-Man is quicker than the ghosts in the early levels and also receives a speed boost known as 'cornering' if the player is able to manoeuvre skilfully around the maze. In Iwatani's only *Pac-Man* sequel that he had direct involvement with, *Pac-Man: Championship Edition*, the player receives a reward, in the form of the 'Sparkster' achievement for turning adeptly. This is a leitmotif of other Namco games, where a corner negotiated with aplomb in *Ridge Racer* is rewarded with a speed boost on exiting the apex. One of the key failures of the technologically superior *Rally-X* was the unfair speed advantage apportioned to the cars which hunted the player's avatar down. For *Pac-Man: Championship Edition*, speed is both a reward, and with the counting down of a clock from five or ten minutes, an essential, perhaps ethical consideration to enter the hallowed spaces and special code of the high score table. As French philosopher Paul Virilio argues, speed is the 'wait for the coming of what abides',[6] as we move quicker, we experience a greater amount of inertia.

This is seen especially in the technologies of speed. They

have a general tendency to reduce the duration (time) between two points (space) and their invention and use are a central feature of the information age and of flexible accumulation more generally. These are technologies which have a specific tendency to *collapse* space twice over: first in decreasing the time taken between departure and arrival, and secondly by illustrating the inverse relationship between the speed of an object and the space available to the incumbent. The air force pilot, the astronaut are both at once moving faster than other heavenly bodies, but are actually unable to move beyond the cockpit that they are secured to in space and time. As long as they remain securely fastened in that life-supported space, they are safe, but any movement outside of it results in risk and the possibility of death. This is not limited to the warfare state, but extends to the welfare state: technologies that are able to prolong life beyond a natural point of departure for body and mind consign individuals to beds bristling with sensors and salves. Patients are unable to move but, strung in a state of suspended animation, are caught between two worlds. The need for speed, for *time extension* which is so essential to Pac-Man, pilot and patient, increases inertia: time can be manipulated, extended, but only through the folding of space.

As the final chapter shows, it is time itself which illuminates the potential exit strategies from this space, yet *Pac-Man* in common with many early videogames was heavily reliant on the folding of spaces, commonly known as 'hyperspace', which allowed the player to take shortcuts, usually behind the screen. These have been variously described as 'warp tunnels', shortcuts, and with deference to an actual place in space and time, the Disney-esque simulacra of 'Wraparound Avenue'.[7] In *Pac-Man*, these form part of a multicursal labyrinth in that there is more than one entrance and exit to the maze. The fact that this space effectively loops back around on itself is instructive of those infinitely generic spaces that we consume as part of the globalised, capitalist experience: it is at once safe in its sameness and stupendous in its smoothness from state to state and country to country. Technologies of speed, the airline and the automobile, operate as hyperspatial links between airports and motorways which are similar in iteration from Africa to Asia.

Numerous McDonald's act as cheap, familiar convenience stops in strange, alien countries so that the body can ingest, digest, defecate or urinate. These generic spaces are signs, symbols and semiotics which comfort as to the primacy of Western spaces and the relations, inert, divorced, human (or otherwise) that they denote and act as an essential part of the centrality of tourism to capitalism discussed in chapter four. Yet when Pac-Man passes behind the maze, the experience of space is the quintessential known unknown: we know that Pac-Man is there, but there is less surety of the experience of travelling through that folded space. This is an experience as individual – and familiar – to the astronaut of the lunar landing, the test pilot and the patient appended in inertia between the existence and demise. All are suspended between life and death, all are instructive of a hyperspace that we are aware of, but have a lack of awareness of the lived (and dead) experience that this entails. Indeed, unless provided with the technology and the opportunity, we are unlikely to experience this with our own body or consciousness until our own end of history.

As with many experiences of the Pac-Man principle, it is at those points where we are totally reliant on technologies that we find ourselves at our most human, at those points where death is not a possibility, but a probability. The closer we are to death, the more alive we feel. In a reversal of the experimentation in safe places that videogames and simulations offer through their technologies, it is expedient to explore the hyperspaces and wraparound avenues behind, above, beyond and below the safe spaces of the game and capitalism. The reterritorialized openings that offer unknown ingress and egress from hypermodern mazes and into classical labyrinths. From the pasteurised and cauterised relations of the motorway, of McDonald's, into those worthy of exploration: bars, boxing rings, the burlesque. These are spaces inscribed with history, the rough walls of stone that drip and leak with the expectation of the future and exploration of past relations. The forests where nature, in its true state, closes in around the walker, where the only trails of traversal are the breadcrumbs or red thread offered by speed of thought exercised under time pressure. These are ghostly spaces, at once alive with the spaces and narratives of the labyrinth, but like the patient or the pilot are filled with the potential for death. Innately, they bridle with the potential for transition, where those haunted by the screen-smooth spaces of capitalism can become the haunter, the dynamics of which are explored in the next chapter.

3

Ghostware: The Hauntologies of *Pac-Man*

As the previous chapter identifies, it is only a change in state, an exploration of spaces and stories not yet properly explored or documented, that enables an alternative path from the hollowed-out, hypermodern spaces privileged by capitalism. Indeed, it is the labyrinth itself, with its access to hyperspaces and strange narratives of the past and present which offer ingress to spaces which are notionally off-limits. Once here, it is up to us to explore and experience these spaces, often through technology, or by entering the hyperspaces where existence is distilled through intense experience, as seen with the reveller on ecstasy, the pugilist in the boxing ring, the reconnoitre of deserted, dilapidated buildings. Even *Pokémon Go* with its augmentation of reality leads the individual outside of the ostensible safe spaces of the game and into the dankest corners of capitalism: an encounter with a Balkan minefield, a cannabis factory and a deserted train track are all possible when looking to catch 'em all. Yet, at the same time the game offers a refreshed and revived interaction with everyday spaces and neighbours and colleagues around us. This, like hyperspace, is a technology suspended between the real and the hyperreal and many armchair travellers like what they see there and enjoy the 'experience'.

Such are the challenges and affordances offered by capitalism. *Pokémon Go*, like *Pac-Man*, is a game which reveals the contradictions at the heart of the model, a place where absolutes are not possible, or even desired. Where the outnumbered and outgunned still have weapons of prophylaxis and the opportunity to turn the tables, given the chance to access symbolic and strange spaces outside, above, beyond and behind the norm. Where a welfare state, so in thrall to the innovation and invention of the technologies of the bottom line of Big Pharma, can still offer hope for the casualty of the technologies of speed, the car or air crash victim, the astronaut suffering from depression: because after outer space there is no inner space left to explore.

To administer and manage such a vast project of capitalism requires equally vast optics of surveillance. Eighteenth century English philosopher Jeremy Bentham imagined the prison, where incarceration was prophylaxis being governed by the 'panopticon'.[1] Yet unlike the US, where the incarceration mantra is 'gotta catch 'em all', the governance and administration of the majority of Western societies falls within being able to 'gotta watch 'em all'. Surveillance of a state which is not at war necessarily extends the notion of the welfare state to protection and prevention based around ensuring insurance and reassurance. Surveillance ensures that personal property (capital) is less likely to be defiled or damaged, reducing insurance claims and threats to the bottom line. At the same time, this reassures the populace that society is safer: increased optics ensure the tautology that only those who have something to hide need have anything to fear from watchful eyes of CCTV, Ofsted, drones, benefits cheats' hotlines and monitoring of electronic communication in the Communications Data Bill. The wider population is reassured that the game being played out in front of these technologies is tactically pure, so that all that information is available to the player at any given time. The question posed by such a delicately poised and technologically sophisticated game is: how is it employed and who can process such information efficiently enough so that the game can be effectively played?

This chapter looks to address this question with recourse to those lovable rogues, the monsters, or ghosts of *Pac-Man* who roam the mazes hour after hour surveying, searching, surveiling for their pie-chart prey. As we will see, for these agents of reconnaissance, there is less emphasis on their proclivity to catch

26

Pac-Man and more about their potential of aiming for a space and time *ahead* of Pac-Man. The is the extension of surveillance through other means including the panopticon and Norwegian sociologist Thomas Mathiesen's extension of this into the 'synopticon',[2] where the many watch the few. This is a concept widely employed in the contemporary freak-shows of reality TV such as *Big Brother* where the audience watching TV watches others who are being watched and, in the case of *Gogglebox*, are actually watching TV.

Alongside the folding of form into content, this infinite flattening out of space using 'big optics' allows 'information from any point [to] be transmitted with the same speed, [so] the concepts of near and far, horizon, distance and space itself no longer have any meaning'.[3] Those who watch the watchers watching enter the realm of French philosopher Grègoire Chamayou's idea of 'drone theory', which, in keeping with playing a tactically pure game, endows us with the potential to be omniscient – if not omnipotent – as 'wide area surveillance' allows us to 'see everything, all of the time'.[4] In the case of *Gogglebox*, this acts as a filter which offers up content which has been preselected by the original broadcasters then sieved through an 'ordinary' person's response to it.

Pac-Man is a videogame which is apportioned with a variety of 'firsts', including being the first in a subtype of games since termed the 'maze-chase' genre; a concerted effort by the developer Toru Iwatani to appeal to wider demographics along with a convergence of videogames with wider popular culture, *Pac-Man* was also the first videogame to include narrative interludes, that is, some semblance of a story as part of its progression. As the previous chapter indicated, at one level this ties in neatly with Borges' conception of the book and the maze being the same thing. Yet at another level it problematises it. The introduction of characterisation, which, in opposition to other videogames of the time such as *Space Invaders*, humanises the relationship between player, Pac-Man and the ghostly apparitions of the monsters, also introduces contradictions to the genealogy of the characters. What is seen as true with Pac-Man in Iwatani's complicated and sometimes incongruous account of the yellow pie-chart's inception in chapter one is at least as true with the family of four ghosts. In a manner befitting their ghostly presence and absence, even their defining predicate of being 'ghosts' appears to have been brought about by their technical disappearance. In the arcade iteration of *Pac-Man*, they were referred to as 'monsters' and were portrayed as such on the cabinet art on the side of the machine. When the game was converted to the Atari Video Computer System home console, the flickering of the sprites due to a lack of processing power led to the monsters being called 'ghosts', thus placing them in a hyperspatial netherworld.

The art of disappearance exhibited by spirits and the spirit of capitalism inspires human culture to yet more inventive and creative ways to remember and revere them: the obsession with the supernatural, of witches, vampires, poltergeists and omen is not because they are there, or even that they are not there, but that they are *nearly* there. The passage into myth is so much easier for the ghostware videogame which is promised a release, but never sees the sheen of the shop's shelf, than the successfully produced title which everyone plays. Absence doesn't always make the heart grow fonder, but it does make the conspiracy stronger: the premature deaths of fabled historical characters from Guy Fawkes to Diana, Princess of Wales, show how conspiracy theories are as tightly wedded to appearance/ disappearance as power and position. A similar ploy is seen in the machinations of the movement of the ghosts of *Pac-Man*, where legend and myth are interspersed with some semblance of reality to provide surprisingly accurate explanations for the apparitions' actions. Like the line of credit which allows the desire of future goods to be realised in consumption in the present, 'ghosts are always thinking one step into the future as they move through the maze'.[5]

Blinky, the first ghost listed on the attract mode of *Pac-Man*, is a prime example of this. His spritely presence and absence apportions him with the character of 'Shadow', with his Japanese equivalent represented by the word *oikake*, translated as 'to run down or pursue'.[6] His tenaciousness is due to the algorithm instructing Blinky to attack the piece of the maze that Pac-Man currently occupies. In this sense, Blinky is a heat-seeking missile. When at a distance from Pac-Man he is reticent to engage, but close by he is hard-wired into homing in on Pac-Man's exhaust, providing the player with the thrill of the chase and giving credence to *Pac-Man* as the first in the genre of 'maze-chase games'. Unlike many contemporary videogames, which become easier as the player progresses due to access to more powerful weapons and levelling up, arcade games of the past would make the game more difficult with progress, impelling the player to insert more coins. *Pac-Man* is no exception, with Blinky concealing a hidden power-up which is contingent on the success of the player.

As the player munches through the dots, pills and spirits of the maze, Blinky is provided with extra speed, turning him into what is commonly known as 'Cruise Elroy'. The origin of this term is unknown, but it is believed to be attributed to Spencer Ouren of the Bozeman Think Tank which cracked the problem of grouping ghosts in *Ms. Pac-Man*.[7] With the term having attained mythical status, there is little surprise to learn that Spencer died in 1992, long before the widespread use of the Internet to foment and ferment speculation, and unfortunately long before he was able to verify the origin of the term, indicating the nonpareil between disappearance and appearance in the production of myth and the questioning of received knowledge, widely seen in the debates around 'post-truth' and 'fake news'.

The speed boost that both Pac-Man and Blinky receive as

they progress through the game are indicative of some of the contradictions which lie at the very heart of the capitalist project. As chapter five discusses, some of these can be seen in recourse to accelerationism. Yet contemporary capitalism is driven by a line of credit which stretches into the future. It impels present desires to be realised without requiring the passage of time and the saving associated with it to pay for them. The proclivity of bringing the future into the present is predicated on the past. This is because only individuals and institutions who are already in debt have access to future lines of credit. This past, present and future artifice of debt must be serviced, if not paid off, to prove that more debt can be 'safely' accrued. Note that the loaning institution is risk free: loans extended to the loanee appear as an asset *not* a liability on the bottom line of the balance sheet. When this leverage is overstretched through loans made against property (so called 'subprime' loans), the lender wraps up high-risk loans with low-risk loans in an easy to swallow power pill of synthetic financial products known as collateralised debt obligations or CDOs. When the loanee stops paying, it is not the physical property of the individual which is protected, but the ghostly ephemerality of capital itself. This is best seen in the 2007–2009 financial crisis where the lender of last resort, the government, through the taxpayer, will always prevent a total financial meltdown. This gaming of numbers, of which we are all complicit, spreads like a contagion from the financial sphere to the welfare state. Schools shimmy a merry dance with Ofsted around education, and hospitals meet NHS's performance metrics whatever the cost to the patient.

In personal lines of credit, similar games are played. Access 0% APR for 18 months on a platinum credit card, then shift the debt to another platinum card before the rate expires, thereby perpetrating an endless circulation of 'free' money through the infinite labyrinth of capital. For those attempting to access credit who are in possession of lower 'metrics', how often is it heard that a credit score, like a high score on an arcade machine, must be improved before a loan can be made? As with a high score, this is a proficiency directly tied to the code of the player's name. On contemporary gaming platforms, this is taken to the end point of its culturally logical conclusion, with 'accounts' piled with points and personal data and validated with (social) capital through a direct and very public relationship to gamer scores. These are boosted through achievements in the game and are placed on the continuum of what Loftus and Loftus, in what may be the first psychological study of videogames, call a 'reward schedule'[8] by winning platinum trophies. The wider use of the reward schedule through gamification is manifest as websites impel the user to share their latest purchase through social media, marking a very definite shift in conspicuous consumption[9] to the online domain.

The advent of this widespread sharing of information demonstrates just how voluntary the contract between wide area surveillance and the individual has become. The mantra is that because there is nothing to hide, all information, from gamerscore to credit score, should both be in plain view and, like money, freely circulated throughout the labyrinth of capitalism. The paradox attaches itself to interaction, like a conspiracy theory to a historical figure, not when something happens and not when something does not happen, but when something *nearly* happens. The near annihilation of the world in the Cuban Missile Crisis of 1962; the near meltdown of the number four reactor at Chernobyl in 1986; the near invoking of the end of history with the collapse of the Berlin Wall in 1989; the near collapse of the financial system in 2008.

In the face of insurmountable odds, it is the *human* spirit which aids the ailing spirit of capitalism: Kennedy and Khrushchev; Ukrainian physicists and engineers; East German revolutionaries; taxpayers. It is precisely the *lack* of an event reaching its culturally logical conclusion which saves capitalism from itself. This is why, in Western societies which seek to attain a post-scarcity utopia, it is *lack* which must be defended. As Benjamin Noys identifies, there is an intrinsic right 'to decommodify our lives',[10] to detach consumerism from the desires of the present being gratified on a continuum of credit built on the artifice of the past. This should not be validated with a self-fulfilling reward schedule of access to an infinite future of free money, but instead with the right to a lack of disclosure of financial, personal and political information to the big optics, a status which the Communications Data Bill (aka 'The Snooper's Charter') which was recently passed into UK law with little or no opposition looks to subjugate and remove. The mantra of the masses, that there is only a problem with surveillance if there is something to hide, is based precisely on this lack and in its reversibility should be taken seriously. This is because the flip side of freedom from surveillance is freedom of speech and similarly, just because there is nothing to say now, it doesn't mean that there won't be in the future.

These are mantras practised – and communicated – at an everyday level via individuals who communicate all the mundane minutiae of their lives. Now, more than ever, with this complicit opening of the masses via their daily data dumps to the ghost hacks and day zero exploits of Government Communications Headquarters (GCHQ), the right to a lack, to omission, to opt out, to be free from surveillance is more vital than ever to the checks and balances that the human spirit provides to the exigencies of capitalism. It is lack which drives the human spirit forwards, questioning, searching, innovating. In filling this lack, markets are used and manipulated through synthetic means in the assimilation and dissemination of scarce resources. Capitalism then seeks to shift beyond, above and behind itself, to *exceed* (as seen in the use of prepositions associated with capital, *sub*prime, *out*source, *off*shore) until it is reversed back on itself and, like Pac-Man gobbled by a monster, self-cannibalises, resulting in its own and humanity's near death. That this has not come to pass is not serendipitous. Necessity, after all, is the progenitor of all invention, but with increasing surveillance of humans, the opportunity to undertake a blindside move, to truly surprise, to symbolically shake the system, is minimised. Capitalism requires humanity not only for its labour, innovation and consumption, but to prevent the worst of the future being realised in the present, so that it acts as a prophylaxis against itself.

The second ghost ghoulishly guesting in the attract mode is Pinky, also known as Speedy, who, in Japanese, is known as *machibuse*, which, as *Pac-Man* expert Jamey Pittman points out in his exhaustive guide, means to perform an ambush.[11] Speedy is not an accurate *nom de guerre* for Pinky, who does not have the hidden accelerative power-up of Blinky, but is, like any good capitalist object, able to fold the future into the present to fuel coping tactics and avoidance strategies on the part of the player. This is achieved by Pinky's algorithm targeting Pac-Man *ahead* of where he currently is in the maze, thus giving the impression of being able to anticipate and therefore lie in wait for Pac-Man.

The tactic used to shake off Pinky is the head-feint, widely used in a host of other games and sports such as basketball and football to give the impression of the ball or the player going somewhere other than the intended target. In *Pac-Man*, this involves popping up from a passage in the maze, moving one way and then darting another, confusing Pinky's algorithm as to where the future Pac-Man might be. As with any tactically pure game, Pinky's information is only as good as the time it is given: so believing Pac-Man to be on an alternative future path is a good way to turn the tables and haunt the haunter. In football, this is known as giving someone the eyes. When Pac-Man chomps down on a ghost after imbibing a power pill, the ghost doesn't die, existing as it does in the present-absence of the spiritual realm, but instead loses its veil, leaving it with just its eyes to guide it back to the den for succour and regeneration. Pac-Man through the head-feint has literally and metaphorically given the capitalist spirit the eyes, following Sun Tzu's *Art of War*[12] in using the strength of the opponent back on itself. The disembodiment of the ghost, firstly as spirit and then as a defeated agent of the beyond, is indicative of the future of surveillance technologies, which by focussing on looking are, by their very nature, fixated on the eyes.

William of Baskerville, the protagonist in Umberto Eco's bestselling semiotic detective story *In the Name of the Rose*,[13] a novel set around a labyrinth library (fittingly overseen by a blind librarian named Borges) in northern Italy employs eyeglasses to read arcane texts, thus technologically augmenting the medieval human being to enhance access to knowledge in an optical drive for information. Optics continue to be appended to the human. The need for progress is complemented by the desire to watch it, to document it. Telescopes were cyclopean in their ability to bring the distant into close proximity, so that in the same way as the spirit of capitalism folds the future into the present, so accompanying human inventions and innovations are able to fold distance into imminence. Safety was ensured through surveillance. Structures were deployed to permit 360° surveillance of the surroundings, allowing some element of control to be exerted over the elements: crow's nests on ships received their name from the use of crows to lead the ship to land when terra firma was beyond visual range, eliding the age-old nautical problem of navigation in inclement weather.

In modernity, structures would be employed to the ends, rather than a means of surveillance, a model of discipline and punishment. Ensuring safety was no longer as straightforward as following the crow as it flies, but complexities and interdependencies meant that there was a requirement of anticipation in exerting control over present and future. This is best seen in English philosopher Jeremy Bentham's 'Panopticon' which, in spite of its architecturally labyrinth construction, conversely allowed the gaoler to oversee a host of inmates from one position. It didn't matter whether the gaoler could actually see the inmate or not, it was the possibility, the presence-absence of *nearly* being watched which was important and disembodies surveillance from tangible space to the abstract space of the mind, evidenced in the concept of the 'internal policeman'. This is the basis for the contemporary use of CCTV surveillance which pervades all of the spaces of the everyday from airports to zebra crossings. The surveilled citizen does not even have to know if a camera is working or not, just that it is nearly there, functioning or not. In the best tradition of the welfare and warfare state of prophylaxis and nuclear strategy, it is deterrence, rather than execution, which is central to effectiveness.

Meanwhile, the solitary watcher, delighting in the dullness, somnambulantly gazes at a multitude of CCTV screens, head fainting with boredom at the closed circuit crow's nests where they watch the multitude go through their day-to-day activities of travelling, eating, consuming and producing. By the time the synopticon of *Big Brother* and *Gogglebox* is realised, all of our heads are fainting, stupefyingly lolling at other individuals who are so inured to cameras and surveillance that there is mass, if interpassive, realisation that wide area surveillance is not only a way of life, but the only way to experience life. Not from behind a lens, or even through one, but in front of one. Its omega point is its appearance on the feed: unless an event is narrowcasted to friends, it is questionable if it ever happened at all. Such are the vagaries of a system predicated on spirits and the haunting of the present where events nearly occur rather than actually take place.

These watching machines of modernity were always connected and attached to the spaces which people pass through, pointing at bodies; interred in the mind, they remained a physical reminder of ensuring insurance through surveillance.

Yet slowly, due to cost and progress, they are becoming obsolete. Now the crow flies, via drone technology, without appendage and restriction through urban and rural spaces. Its first instance use is morally ambivalent given drones have been used for military applications for decades, before being deployed in the asymmetrical war on terror. Yet drones are equally proficient at saving people who are drowning in remote water and to illuminate a safe way through darkened areas.

They have a light-hearted element too, with drones used for leisure flights by enthusiastic amateurs and, as Chamayou notes, record vistas of awe-inspiring scenery, thus resurrecting the possibility of an eternal return of technology to its playful and emancipating potential.[14] Yet these drones perhaps embody – or disembody – the spirit of capitalism more than any contemporary technology. They are the floating eyes of ghosts, able to traverse between and through buildings, ethereal, omniscient, they can see without being seen, kill without being killed and, with their ability to stay airborne for hours without the requirement for expensive and heavy life support systems for the human meat of pilots, physically dispel the need for skilled pilots. In fact as Chamayou reinforces throughout his excellent *Drone Theory*, their operators approach flying the drone in the same way as a dedicated arcade player would approach mastery of a game. Like a game, impelling the gamer to 'insert coin', the experience inures a strange sense of codependency. Just as Pac-Man relies on the ghosts for meaning, so the operator comes to depend on their prey: 'surveillance may last for weeks while the operators are shadowing their targets. They follow them in all their daily occupations, sometimes even to the point of developing a strange sense of intimacy with them'.[15] It is strikingly similar to the guides (see chapter six) employed in mastering *Pac-Man*. Each pattern is worked through, recorded, noted, reworked. It is *observed, surveilled*. By marking out historical movements of their target, the game as a means of being able to anticipate the future is assured, until one day, with the patterns of the quotidian firmly committed to memory, the prey are eradicated, the high score attained and the game completed, its achievement committed to electronic and human memory like a gamerscore and a playguide.

Yet it is precisely this intimacy, based on spatial, if not temporal, proximity which leads to a host of pathologies, rising from the disembodiment of warfare into something ephemeral, sublimated. For the drone, writes Chamayou, is a weapon with no body.[16] Drone operators suffer from a withdrawal and disconnection from everyday life which are, sadly, intensifications of the spectrum of mental illnesses which accompany post-industrial capitalism. This cultural logic, having conquered the outer spaces of the environment, looks to populate the inner spaces of the mind, the result of which, as philosopher Bernard Stiegler argues, is a pharmacological society based on treating the very mental illnesses that the exigencies of the spirit of capitalism cause in the human spirit. Stiegler observes the same disconnection of the *otaku* and *hikkomori* in Japanese society, who, lost in a 'closed, virtual world' of electronica and fantasies of their own construction, withdraw into a disaffection[17] away from normal life.

Otaku and *hikkomori* mirror those deeply introspective and melancholic experiences of drone operators who encounter a pure warzone which is at once both close and distant, meaning that 'it is like living in two places at the same time'.[18] It is paradoxical to think that the drone operators, whose ontology is based almost entirely on the surveillance of bodies, do not appear to inhabit their own. Like the ghosts of *Pac-Man*, the poltergeists of the paranormal, the spirits of capitalism, the litany of conspiracy theories, the events of history, all are predicated on not quite being there, of not quite being fully realised. This means that the human spirit is susceptible to all of these excesses.

Existing somewhere between the physical world and the

mental world, but always surveilled, the human spirit needs to take on the appearance of the most difficult ghost to avoid in *Pac-Man*. Inky, who with his uneven temper and erratic behaviour acts like he is either ill or in the Japanese translation of *kimagure* 'of uneven temper'.[19] In this sense it is only acts which are fickle, unheralded and unanticipated which can become events. These are not the pseudo events of the release of a film, or videogame, or carefully surveilled attendance at football matches, but the symbolic, unexpected: the stolen kiss, a bonfire on the beach, a food fight in the mess, the rejection of anti-depression medication. Those things which carry emotion and meaning to the individual and wider world, those things, which either before, during or after, make us feel like Inky's *nom de guerre* 'bashful': not because it was something that we did, but because it was something we couldn't believe that we did. Not that nearly happened, but actually happened. This is the negation of the art of disappearance and it is a strategy beyond the excesses of the haunted spirit of the nearly-happenings of capitalism.

4

The Politics of Pac-Land

The philosophy of surveillance is to eradicate threats before they are executed. It is the prophylaxis of terrorism, wrapped in a tautology: if an act can be anticipated it will not take place. The precrime of *Minority Report* is brought to bear not on individuals, but on entire societies. Like the nuclear umbrellas projected by the US during the Cold War, the warfare state is the cost of the benefit of the welfare state, that protection can only be ensured through protectionism. Like moving through the videogame, where checkpoints offer a haven of safety and permit the saving of a current favourable state of play, individuals move through airports, parsing documents, reading retinas, submitting fingerprints. Safety as surveillance, the speed of control an addiction which relies entirely on the control of speed. (Nation) states are saved from terrorism before it occurs. Such is the passive glumness of the modern traveller that it is no wonder that all aeronauts are called passengers: there is a repressive resignation that the submission of bio-political information are things that are done to us, not for us. Pseudo-paramilitary personnel oversee every sad queue ensuring maximum compliance and minimum dissension, leading Paul Virilio to observe, dramatically, but accurately, that 'airports have the tragic nature of concentration camps'.[1] The individual looks to negotiate the humans with guns and the homogeneity of McDonald's in airports to access to the gifts of globalisation, food, alcohol, weather, language, narcotics, love: culture. The light-touch totalitarianism is, everyone tells themselves, a small price to pay.

Taito's *Operation Wolf* (1987) spotlights Virilio's observation perfectly. The objective of the game is for the one-man army who is sent on a plausibly deniable mission to an unnamed south-east Asian country (Vietnam) to liberate hostages and airlift them to safety. *Operation Wolf* plays fast and loose with human life. The screen scrolls around villages in the jungle and ammo dumps, armed locals who pop up on to the screen like a digital *Whack-a-Mole* are dispatched with joyous aplomb via the life-size Uzi submachine gun bolted to the cabinet. It is not the genre of game that is telling (Wikipedia lists it as a 'shooting gallery', rather than 'first person shooter'), but the content. The player is in tourism mode, the scenery cruising by as if from the window of a tram or jeep, picking off the heterogeneous opposition who dare to spoil the view of the vista.

The final two levels of *Operation Wolf* are called 'Concentration Camp' and 'Airport' respectively. The pairing of two of the 20th century's most awesome totalitarian technologies does not appear to be by accident. The intensification of speed, seen in the mass transit system of the aeroplane, is a concentration of speed. The arrival at the concentration camps of Oświęcim by train is, quite literally, the terminal, the end of everyday life, an unarguable terminus of life. For the tourist at the airport, the terminal represents the concentration of speed and the willing submission to totalising processes that are part of a change from everyday life to the exotica of the beyond. Both groups, in the airport and the concentration camp, will submit to any measures to survive, hand over papers, get undressed in front of uniformed personnel, have personal effects confiscated. Their sullen silhouettes, draped by a thousand hangdog shoulders, are testament to the Pac-manic need to survive at any cost, to see what is beyond the end, beyond the terror of the terminal.

The airport terminal provides a vista on to the global threat of terrorism. It is not founded on political totalitarianism, where entire societies are subjugated, but instead on the homogenising effects of tourism, instigated at the local, often individual level. Tourists will carry these effects, like a virus, unwittingly, but rarely unwillingly. Instead of transferring themselves to another culture, there is a tendency to transfer their culture with themselves. Accordant technological and economic improvements are demanded – and implemented – without question and without due care on to the host culture. Expectations rise, with a focus on what is believed to be 'real' understood in relation not to the space of their hosts, but to their own experiences of home: 'What is that in real money?' 'What's the real time?' This appears to connect with a recently revised narrative of neo-colonial soft power favoured by Anglo-Saxon countries where the English language is utilised as the vehicle of export, but is probably more akin to leaving litter at a picnic spot, where the Styrofoam cup which blanches in the sun and rolls in the wind is at the whim of nature, but refuses to integrate with it.

Cultural theorist Gerry Coulter[2] notes that the tourism mode is precisely how the hypermodern and hypermobile terrorist operates. The very same techniques of cells and networks which are used to make up the Western world's awesome and terrible communication technologies from concentration camps to airports are favoured by the sleeper cells and terror networks of terrorists. They are just as conversant with the mass systems of caves in Helmand as the aviation, money, media and computer nodes of the West. In the law of reversibility taken to its logical conclusion, on September 11th 2001 the mass media broadcast to the watching masses the signs of mass trade being obliterated by massive vehicles of mass transport placed in the sky as part of a desire for mass tourism. Tourism, from the screen to the aeroplane and all means of communication in between, inverts into terrorism. Freedom, for whatever it was worth, would never be the same again, seen in how mass tourism then became subject to the same controls that were previously extended to terrorists. If tourism is the Pac-Man wondering and wandering through homogenised, but still faintly alien spaces, the terrorist is the ghost that haunts, traps and kills within the same system.

If the life of the consumer, as Polish sociologist and holocaust survivor Zygmunt Bauman reminds us, is 'first and foremost about being on the move',[3] Pac-Man is not only the quintessential consumer, but also the apogee of tourism. Movement is not only expected, but demanded, in leisure as well as toil. Therefore, the Pac-player, like Pac-Man, does not suffer from a lack of freedom, but too much, even if that is structured and concentrated towards terminals and goals. Freedom is everywhere, hypodermic in its hyphenation 'free-trade deal', 'duty-free', 'tax-free', 'free-trade zone', 'interest-free', 'tariff-free free-trade zone'. The ubiquity of the hyphen, as German philosopher Herbert Marcuse muses, means that terms 'designating quite different spheres or qualities are forced together into a solid, overpowering whole'.[4] The proclivity for hyphenated language to fuse terms permits astoundingly contradictory political statements to be uttered with little awareness or dissent from a largely myopic electorate, who, like the same-styled Pac-labyrinth, airport or shopping centre, only see political parties and rule through the lens of one slightly different iteration from one manifestation to the next.

This is homogenisation on an industrial scale. It carries through to the global system, where capitalist democracy is the one and only model: it is as if politics and economics became stuck in the early 20th century Fordist production model of having one colour as long as it is black, reflected in the ongoing attempts to control speed and totalise society. Ironically, this stagnation ensures a general stability in globalised (Western) politics. Even as the crises of capitalism have piled upon one another, in a kind of Faustian pact, politicians are permitted to carry on with their tasks, as long as the populace are permitted to consume. Politics becomes the hell of the same. Individuals will not ask for anything more than more of the same. A free, but monomanic choice in politics is acceptable as long as there remains a free, but monocultural choice in the consumer society.

Therefore, freedom in this context, of hyphens and tautologies, is not wedded to the idea of political democracy, but to the ideal of bureaucratic trade and capital, with regulations and determinations in place to ensure that freedom is assured at all costs. The war *against* terror was pitched as a battle *for* freedom. In meeting all needs and wants, the utopia of Western capitalist democracies is achieved, but the tragic nature of the airport is replicated across entire societies. This is not enforced with guns, but tacit agreement between entire swathes of the population and politicians that there will be no dissension or deviance from an ideal freedom, in a 'pattern of one dimensional thought and behaviour',[5] which is founded on the ideal one dimensional individual.

At the level of terrorism, the end point, the final destination, is the suicide bomber or solitary gunman, who, like a single player or Pac-Man himself, acts alone, 'a lone wolf', seen in the Westminster terror attack of 2017. These are one-dimensional individuals, representative of and enabled by the global networks of commerce and communication, religion and resistance which allowed them to concentrate their efforts to being the terminal of other people's lives. It is the technologies of transport that are used for this, the signs of being on the move: aeroplanes in 2001; trains in 2004; tube trains in 2005; trucks in 2016; cars in 2017. For most, who never reach this self-determining act, we move through circuits of space, consuming, touring, travelling and working, vaguely aware of threat, but like Pac-Man, not allowing the spectre of terror to deviate us from the next need, the imminent purchase, the subsequent holiday getaway.

The terrorist is the tourist taken to its logical conclusion. A risk and a trip undertaken in search of an afterlife that is contingent on reaching the terminal point. How does politics respond to this? For politicians and politics, it is not power which is the overriding motivation, but lack of relevancy. Avoiding falling away from sight is Pac-Man avoiding the ghost in the maze: Theresa May is the apogee, ghostly, vacant but always present, as long as the politician stays alive, stays in view, but tantalisingly out of sight, they remain in tourism mode. Each voter, like the visitor to a foreign country, can see the results of their preferences in the clashes between leaders in news and current affairs programmes. Looking through the screens of television or windows of monitors, the voter has an abstract notion of control, which is almost a simulation. Lacking the immediate response of the videogame, they remain in fugue state as to the effect of their vote, captured by the language used by politicians, which in its hyphenated tautologies captures the wants and needs of the electorate.

It is not the politicians who are tourists, pulled to foreign climes on a phantom expenses account, but the electorate gazing through a one-dimensional screen at a one-dimensional politics, the chambers and halls of power similar to the ancient labyrinths of classicism and steeped walkways of libraries. Viewing the Houses of Parliament is exactly the same as being on a package holiday for pensioners. People walk around in costumes, alcohol is imbibed with impunity, the locals are bemused, the buildings require restoration and bewildered locals shout at each other.

The rub in politics arises when a totalising system of control and one dimensionality meets the soft, human underbelly of the politician who is largely motivated by the need to introduce goodness to society and eradicate evil. The often-maligned Conservative party of 2010–2016 was perhaps the worst offender of trying to do good. Perpetually stuck in what Jean Baudrillard calls 'referendum mode',[6] politics takes on the shape of a *Pac-Man* arcade game that can't quite boot up properly and is caught in a Möbius loop of testing and retesting to see where the problem lies. An obsession with this testing, seen in the NHS and throughout the education system, spread like a virus to the political realm. Constant testing did not highlight what was going right, but what was going wrong. It was not power that was addictive in this sense, but what was irrelevant. If as Baudrillard notes, 'tests and referenda are, as we know, perfect forms of simulation: the question induces the answer, it is *designated* in advance' and are an ensconced binary system of question and answer signals,[7] then it is only by asking more questions, by having more polls, by going to the political tourists, who after all ventured only very occasionally to the booth to participate in democracy, more often that politicians and politics can find out what individuals really want.

The motivation here is reason and being reasonable. This becomes like a power pill in that more information can be found out by asking more questions. Yet, over time, the power of reason becomes the 'sleeping pill of the mind',[8] before taking on the manifestation of a drug. The power pill, instead of chasing away the nasty little ghosts of the totalitarian past, becomes an addiction to reason and rationality within itself.

The warning signs were there from early on. David Cameron's party was aligned at the political centre, with a constant emphasis on reasonableness, enshrined in the heir-to-Blair aphorism 'call me Dave'. True to his commitment to the Liberal Democrat part of the coalition, Dave provided a referendum on alternative voting. The tourist population, rarely asked for its opinion, looked on to the windows of Westminster with detached bemusement and the status quo of the first-past-the-post voting model was maintained. To demonstrate how willing the Conservatives were to be reasonable and to show the tourists that their power and politics was not one dimensional, a further referendum was given to Scotland to decide on independence from the United Kingdom of Great Britain and Northern Ireland in 2014. The entire political capital of the Conservative cabinet was predicated on this. In an early warning, polling suggested that it was going to be closer than the eventual 55%-45% split in favour of remaining as part of the Union. The real problem arose when pollsters were certain throughout the 2015 general election campaign that the Labour party would win: they didn't. The Conservative's centre politics, based in and around the referendum mode, attained a new and unexpected high score and an increased parliamentary majority in the House of Commons.

In many ways, the Conservatives were giving the population exactly what they wanted, the exercise of choice in politics as well as in shopping. The extension of testing from public services to service to the public. It is effectively market research undertaken in the real time of the referendum. If, as Baudrillard contends, the answer – or response – is always embedded in the question, then the voting population, who were becoming repeat visitors to the political realm, could always be relied upon to give the correct – or at least politically expedient in terms of the one-dimensional status quo – outcome to the yes/no binary. As much as the ruling political party were reasonable, so the view through the tourist/ referendum mode could be seen to be reasonable too. Yet the power pill, as Bauman reminds us, although initially used as a force for good, to extend good, with extended use over a period of time and in 'large doses, turns into poison'.[9]

This occurs because these questions, like the majority of questions posed in the Pac-Land of one-dimensional society, belong to the category of safety of maintaining an effective status quo. Constant referenda become risky with their reason. Whilst the occasional drug may help with sleep, to keep the tourists somnambulant on their long flight through the excesses of 21st century utopia, constant use is dangerous and rational faculties are overawed. With the advent of the 2016 referendum on membership of the European Union, it was both the voting population and the politicians, all of whom were long inured into the referendum/tourism mode, who lost their faculties and started acting like hallucinating soldiers on the Vietnam front line. Individual voters, who long felt disenfranchised from travelling in the same transnational corridors and networks as the rest of the globalised set, were set upon a voyage of tourism which quickly transformed into terrorism. Viewing the interactions of this foreign body of politicians, there was a realisation that what was said could matter, quite apart from the usual hyphenated banalities of politics. Politicians, long seen as an elite who were not believed by voters, were openly saying things that even they themselves did not believe. They were seen not one dimensionally, not as people who spoke in closed hyphenated banalities, but as open oxymorons. For those apparently disenfranchised, those who were not tourists to the fruits of globalisation, but had seen holidaymakers to the UK become permanent citizens, this was a rare opportunity to be a tourist in the first instance and terrorist in the endgame.

Like learning to play a videogame well, each game a test of the skills that are inculcated into an individual to allow them to thrive in a new post-industrial economic meritocracy, so the referendum, in its binary opposition as a test and triggers 'response mechanisms in accordance with stereotypes or analytical models'[10] which is embedded in every media, is a vine running through digital societies and elicits a certain media response. This was seen in the vindicated fervour from the right, veracious remorse from the left, and was a stereotypical output: the blame firmly attributed to the other. Politics for that time was no longer one dimensional, but two dimensional; there was the possibility that the tourists had terrified the terra firma of the referendum mode. This made the referendum on the UK's membership of the European Union, simulation though it appeared to be, designated in advance as it should have been, the first real political event that had happened in and to the UK for decades. The lolling agape disbelief of David Cameron's slack-jaw a Pac-look into the labyrinth of negotiation and bureaucracy the UK will face over the coming decades.

In this case the referendum, prefigured on the binary choice of yes/no, on/off, I/O, 1/0, revealed the binary divide in the UK. The global and the local. Those who would pay the price for the networks of tourism and 'freedom' and those who never even felt the one-dimensional freedom of Pac-Land. In spite of the stereotypes framed in the media, this is not precluded on the divide between rich and poor: as a capitalist democracy, the utopian system always already provides widescreen TVs to play the latest videogames on, the best pay-TV to watch and the fastest food to eat. After all, this is the key criticism of the unemployed, that they don't work for all of the goodies that they have within arm's reach of the remote control lost down the back of the overstuffed leather sofa. Instead, the referendum/tourism mode is closer to how Jean Baudrillard frames the execution of terror in his provocative *The Spirit of Terrorism*. The act of terrorising the current status quo is 'what particularly frightens us, they have become rich, without ceasing to wish to destroy us'.[11] The constant refrain from the left of the 'poor' voting against their own best interests is enshrined in these tourists-terrorists who 'in terms of our own system of values, they are cheating. It is not playing fair to throw one's own death into the game'.[12]

It seems flippant, blithe, and even perhaps insulting to the memories of those that die in terrorist acts to say that a bloodless referendum can be placed within the same frame of reference as the terrorist attacks which have taken innocent lives without discrimination or discernment. Yet it is not the quantifiable death, damage or devastation that is visited upon the system that is most telling, but as the creation of *Pac-Man* instructs, it is found in the symbolic act. For the attack on the architecture of the Twin Towers, themselves the literal and metaphysical manifestation of one-dimensional society with their binary reflective symmetry of 1/1, carried out on 01/11 (or 11/01) was symbolic. Following the attacks, weaponised from within the capitalist system of nodes, cells and networks, capitalism itself no longer possessed the same on/off binary, or a lack of choice. Similarly, after a tourist trip through the referendum mode of the West's one-dimensional society, where an addiction to reason, to faith in that most capitalistic of acts, the outsourcing of power, showed that radical change only comes from within the system itself, there is a concurrent realisation that the second, hidden dimension of society is symbolic. Now, the ghosts are out of the pen, chasing down the drug-addled, gape-mouthed, exhausted Pac-politician. From Whitehall to the White House, there is a requirement to go back in time to accelerate into the future.

5

Accelerate Your Mind: The Soundscapes of *Pac-Man*

Pac-Man, the simple symbolic 'kuchi' whose broad appeal lies in the straightforward life of eating *ad nauseam*, betrays the disputed genealogy of his creation seen in chapter one. This contention reveals an abrasion between creativity and technology; as games scholar Mark JP Wolf identifies, early instances of graphics within the videogame were artistically limited and relied on visual representations that were relatively abstract[1] employing geometric, symmetrical shapes that were easily identifiable. From the moustachioed *Mario* to the Monty Python-esque wind-up ducks of *Manic Miner*, these images are a reminder of the origins of what videogame historian Steven L. Kent terms the first quarter (1975–2000) of commercial videogame history.[2]

The use of such graphics as a key part of their content is allied with their close technological relationship with visual media from the cathode ray tubes of oscilloscopes and monitors through to the LCDs and LEDs of mobile devices and televisions. Videogames are therefore widely perceived as an audio-visual medium. Yet the audio aspect is often overlooked in favour of graphical accomplishment. This is in spite of their incipient (along with physical and social) positioning in amusement arcades where the soundtrack to an ebullient cash-rich industry was high on its own supply of the chinging of coins, machine attract modes and hollers of defeat and victory. Machines provided the soundtrack to the win/loss rhythm of coin insertion, button press, duel/dual with the machine and eventual triumph or agony.

Early videogames, monoliths of the arcade, their cyclopean monitors fixated on the pockets of punters normally drawn to the flatbed of pinball machines, set much of the precedent for eliding the audio in lieu of the visual. Pinball was a mating ritual. The player had their hands on the hips of the machine, nudging the table in response to the winks of the lights, the coaxing of rubber bumpers, tapping the right buttons to attain the reward of the chiming of a bell, or the soft chunk of the rubber bumpers. Allurement worked and was rewarded, but the exercise of too much power and anger would tilt the table meaning that the game of seduction was up. Meanwhile, early videogame arcade machines were vertical, the player caught in a coital dance with a machine taller and more foreboding, the monitor reflecting on to flickering faces peering into the black hole before them. Who knows what the player was seeing, let alone hearing? Yet, the menacing artwork of the monsters of *Space Invaders* was metaphorically and practically correct: this was the era of science fiction, of the post-industrial, where leisure, pleasure, work and toil would be focussed on the ubiquitous screen, shallow in its dimensions, infinite in its information.

Both types of machine are examples of Marshall McLuhan's observation that games can have 'neither meaning nor existence except as extensions of our immediate inner lives'.[3] If early audio-visual iterations of pinball such as *Pong* were relatively dour in their monochrome presentation, then their sound effects were equally binary and did not compete with the bumpers and lights of pinball, whose electromechanical ratcheting and banging were a glorious orgy of Fordist industrialism and boomer optimism. Yet still people flocked to *Pong*, drawn, like a flickering character on the TV screen, through a culture educated, entertained and explained through broadcast television. Late blooming boomers and progenic Gen Xers were caught between the organisation of time seen in the schedules of TV listings and the possibilities of the postmodern, to earn extension, in work, in education, in healthcare, not by earning extra balls as with pinball, but by earning extra credit, to extend their confidence in their own future.

This is a confidence bought and borrowed, not earned. The iconicity of '1UP' applies just as certainly to the competitive arena of conspicuous consumption ('one-upmanship') as to the picking up of extra lives in a game. Indeed, in the pay-to-play economic model of post-industrial capitalism this allows additional lives to be lived. As with *Pac-Man*'s power pills there were parallel upgrades which offered better education, better healthcare, more wives, faster cars, late-opening bars, longer lives, extended play. It seems almost inevitable that this generation would find themselves suspended, caught between the certain industrial rigour of the past and the uncertain possibility of the future, and thereby perceived as slackers, their inertia mistaken for inaction.

The prevalence of mechanical, electromechanical and electronic machines in amusement arcades makes them a very public display of what sociologist Peter Freund calls the 'technological habitus'[4] where the rhythms of a highly technical and rationalised world imbue the human body and alter our relationship to wider society. It is seen at an everyday level when the body, inured to hearing the shrill chirrup of the alarm clock, wakes up before it goes off, or the involuntary spasm of the hand as an email burrs into an inbox. The body's inclination for sleep, food, defecation and sex are flexed around deadlines, timetables and targets, meaning that the simple things in life, things that are the hallmark of Pac-Man's existence, symbolically enshrined at the bodily level in the multiple openings of 'kuchi' are elided in the technological habitus.

Amusement arcades are the audio-visual technological habitus par excellence. By shutting out natural light, they have no relationship to time and space outside of their own dank caverns. They are instead illuminated by artificial light from above and below and their monetary soundtracks of score and credit chime with the expectation that the body will insert coin into the machines in exchange for a waggle of the 'joystick', thus joining the coitus between human and machine. It is in this sci-artifice of the amusement arcade where the true space to be invaded is unveiled. The body. Rhythms of the technological habitus are absorbed, leaching between what Freund terms the 'seams in the cyborg',[5] a human/machine tango where scheduled time is scheduled on the trajectory of Moore's Law, where the speed of semiconductor technology doubles every 12–18 months. Instead of this law of acceleration being applied solely to silicon semiconductors, it extends into and through the cyborg indicating an interminable trajectory of the body in society as everything accelerates. This is the case even when – or especially when – a greater number of bodies are inert and suffering from the maladies of obesity, back pain and heart disease associated with it: as the planet speeds up we end up as orbital bodies, observing the world through screens, from afar.

Space Invaders offers an entrance to the arcade on many levels. Like *Pac-Man*, the characters, in this case aliens creeping across the screen, were simple abstractions and remain one of the medium's most enduring images. Taito's machine was prophetic in name too as Japan's technological supremacy touched down in Western amusement arcades, demonstrating how America's commitment to an umbrella of welfare and warfare across the world was working back on its own nexus of industrial power. Japan had been so thoroughly reformed and rehabilitated into the American way that it was able to offer American products and inventions such as calculators, microcomputers and wristwatches in cheaper and more efficient iterations. This social, economic and cultural foray became a familiar narrative of American films of the 1980s which feared the changes that technological automation wrought to the industrial heartlands, lamented in the passing of the industrial society in *Gung Ho* and the cyborg future imperfect of *Blade Runner*.

Less noted, however, is the panic that *Space Invaders* imbues at the bodily level. In common with Mark JP Wolf's observation of the link between graphical low fidelity, abstraction and characterisation, music games scholar Karen Collins finds that it is a *lack* of technology which is key to the creative process in music and sound.[6] This leads to *Space Invaders'* simple four note bassline being widely perceived as one of the first examples of in-game music and certainly the first to evidence a dynamic soundtrack: as the alien invasion comes ever closer, the music speeds up, panicking the player into more frantic and less accurate blasting.

This propensity to panic is given further urgency by the source of this soundtrack. As Gary Western writes, both Taito's *Space Invaders* and its Atari competitor *Asteroids* used heartbeat-like rhythms for their soundtracks.[7] The soundtrack starts slowly, more languid than the player's own biorhythms of the heart, relaxing, coaxing, like the baby feeling rather than hearing the heart of the mother in the womb. As the game progresses, the rhythmic thrumming speeds up, matching the resting cadence of the player who is invested in the game, but is still in control, keeping the aliens at bay and asteroids at arm's length. By defeating these enemies, the game should become easier, but the inverse occurs. As the number of enemies reduces, the game – and the music – speeds up. Partly this is a technical consideration. With less processing power required for the number of on-screen graphics, visual movement – along with the soundtrack – can be accelerated.

The accelerated rhythm of the machine is inverse for the human in the cyborg. There are fewer enemies, so less threat, yet the body, the 'meat', struggles to adapt to acceleration and reacts in a primal, Pavlovian manner, the internal human biorhythms of cardiovascular stimulation apparent, quick, shallow breathing, perspiration, dilated pupils: an acceleration of the body, even when effectively physically inert, mimicking the machine's internal computation processes. Invariably the strength and pace of the heartbeat rises. It is a contradictory response, but keeping up is the only thing the machine requires of the human, yet it is the one thing the body struggles to do. This is also seen at the very limits of techno-capital. Complex financial instruments, 'high frequency trades', which operate 'somewhere below the horizon of human perception and close to the speed of light'[8] with intrinsic vertical risk/reward schedules, mean that it is almost impossible for a human to observe, let alone predict, the vector of the machine. The processor's own heartbeat is the hum of white noise, which, like the languorous, slow intro of *Space Invaders* and *Asteroids*, lulls the body to sleep in security, leaving only the sci-artifice of the machine on cyclopean watch. Artificial intelligence.

These very human bodily responses to the stimulation of the machine are also inverse and contradictory. Steady streams of white noise are widely used (and remediated/simulated through apps) to send the body to slumber in darkened rooms. Meanwhile, the synthetic stimulants of speed and ecstasy were used to keep the body up with late jungle techno's insistence on 180 beats per minute. The converse position of the body imbues comedian Marcus Brigstocke's now legendary utterance 'If *Pac-Man* had affected us as kids, we'd all be running around in dark rooms, munching pills and listening to repetitive electronic music'[9] with a new meaning beyond the caverns of music and comedy clubs, amusement arcades and snooker halls.

In Iwatani's 'true' sequel to the original *Pac-Man*, 2007's *Pac-Man: Championship Edition*, the legacy of *Asteroids* and *Space Invaders* and the influence of powder, pills and power-ups in darkened rooms is apparent in the championship course of Highway II. Beginning with the ditty from the 1980 original, the player is counted into a 'time-attack' game of five minutes in which to amass as many points as possible. A large timer at the top of the screen counts down towards zero hour with the graphics infused with the neon psychedelia common to clubs and caverns. The chief aim is to wake up as many of the slumbering ghosts as possible to follow Pac-Man around the maze and organise them in a compressed kill-chain,[10] which in military parlance means reducing the amount of time to 'eyes-on' target.

Like drone warfare, this is an exercise undertaken at the limits of capital, a game of raw, rational efficiency, tied to the technological habitus. Patterns are tried and retried to short-cut the maze, the meat in the cyborg micro-twitching in response to the stimuli of the game. Inert. Hyper-stimulated. Note the player of *Pac-Man*. They do not look at where the character is currently on-screen, but instead are focussed somewhere *ahead* of the game, in a future space and time that Pac-Man will occupy. This is living in an accelerated future, the body adjusted and adapted: race face on, eyes on the prize. That constant focus on the imminent: 'If I can just have this new phone, I will be happy, if I can achieve promotion, I can even pay for it…'

Death is the enemy. Capital cannot extract capital from dead playbour. So it is in-game. Even one death to Pac-Man means top score potential is obliterated and the body rabidly restarts the level, counter reset, kill-chain futures recalibrated. The ambience of the cavern is filled with the liquid darkness of the techno dance track, whose initial sound effects are a slow heartbeat permeated by the echoes of water dropping through a cave. Increased processing power of contemporary hardware means that there is no need for acceleration to be extracted from technical limitations. Instead, a counter at the bottom of the screen details the elevating speed of the game. This counter kicks up as the timer ticks down; as more points are amassed, the potential amount of points available to the player journeying through the maze increases, in accelerating the future risk/reward schedule. The music intensifies its urgency, a soundtrack to the speed and pills and fruit, the slumbering nether-bodies of the ghosts awoken by a passing-Pac-Man, incessantly chasing down their prey, praying for an opportunity to eat as he does.

When there are enough ghosts in the kill-chain, the pursued

Pac-Man turns his head and chows down on the ghosts, scores doubling, tripling, quadrupling as each melodic munch reverberates through the cavern, recombining with the bassline of the ambient acid audiovisuals. With each ghost consumed there is a distant realisation that these enemies without bodies, the bodies without organs, are perhaps closer to this new accelerated humanity than even Marcus Brigstocke's quick quip is apt to admit. Finally as the music reaches a frenetic climax, the player's score is displayed on the screen, followed by line graphs and bar charts, in a final accession to capital's predilection for measuring everything in quantitative data, the language of the machine.

The long-term influence of the rhythms of music and amusement arcades is taken to its lowest common denominator in the mid-late 1990s' prevalence of rhythm action games, which can still be seen today in variant forms alongside fruit machines in seaside arcades in the UK. Bizarrely, they even make an appearance in the future as one of the few forms of entertainment available to Chris Pratt and Jennifer Lawrence's characters in sci-artifice film *Passengers*. Yet Brigstocke's aphorism is a Lydian stone of the past optimism of 1980s and 1990s counterculture, which sequestered itself away in spaces where the technological habitus was most pervasive. These were quasi-private arenas designed around rational techniques and machines, where nature and natural rhythms were held in abeyance: out-of-town shopping centres, amusement arcades, subways, snooker halls. Even bedrooms, a personal refuge from the world for so many teenagers, became infused and then enthused with the possibilities presented by the music of Detroit techno and the home computers of Spectrum and Commodore. The former's influence was realised in rave, then jungle, and its infamous inclusion in the 1994 Criminal Justice Act which ruled against the prevalence of 'repetitive beats' at spontaneous dance events. The latter's sway begot a generation of 'bedroom coders' who would design, program, produce and publish videogames from the solitary confines of their bedrooms.[11] A young Richard D. James, who would later be known as Aphex Twin, drew on both of these influences to produce sound on a Sinclair ZX81 microcomputer, even though it lacked any built-in sound hardware. He won £50 for his efforts and these hybrid influences of computers and music continued to inspire his future ambition, with the musician admitting in 2004 that: 'I always wanted to make my music sound like a game. A danceable version of a Spectrum game'.[12]

In 1992 he may have come closest to realising this aspiration when he released his EP *Pac-Man* under the alias 'Power Pill'. A glutinous jungle bassline is overlaid by samples from the 1980 arcade game with the song impelling the listener/player/user to 'insert coin' (presumably buy pills from a dealer), before 'eating them [pills] up yum yum'. For proponents of accelerationism, there are two instances at work here. First, the tendency for jungle to utilise samples from the sci-artifice of the technological habitus is indicative of a shift of the human towards the limits of capitalism, which, as Noys observes, traces this 'future inhuman state'.[13] Second is the requirement for the body to be augmented through chemical synthetics to maintain time with this acceleration at the limits: ecstasy and speed push the carcass into a hyper-stimulated state akin to the panic of *Asteroids*, an experience of 'extinction through exhilaration'.[14] Prefiguring capitalism under accelerationism, the body in the throes of speed and ecstasy operating in arrhythmia goes beyond its boundaries. Eventually it crumples in comedown from the pills and powder, rendering the human as just another ghost lolling in the corner suffering from E-flu.

Like the Pac-player, gazing at a time and space ahead of the character, the body in this state is a veteran of the future. The body of the dance floor, like the Pac-player, is simultaneously inert and hyper-stimulated. Shifting epileptically, the body moves in one place whilst the mind journeys to the outer limits of the urban jungle, at once in a state of deep rhythm with the machine, yet deep arrhythmia and dissatisfaction with the current epoch, where the body no longer fits. At this transitional, liminal point, where capitalism present and future is embedded, physically *embodied*, the past/present is seen as human and the present/future as posthuman. On the comedown, the individual is witness to the vagaries of the capitalist project: the black market providing drugs which are unregulated, untried, untested, like experimental weapons of the battlefield. The locations of the raves themselves are a battlefield, the revellers versus the police simulating past battles between the police and the National Union of Miners in Yorkshire and Nottinghamshire. Yet this is a conflict pitched on individual production and consumption, of the technological habitus of production of music in bedrooms, where videogames, bootlegged tapes, vinyl and rave flyers lie on top of one another.

Temporarily missing in action, the body has returned, e-xhausted. In a word, spent. There seems to be little coincidence that the music which inspired *Pac-Man Championship Edition*'s soundtrack found its inception in the Rust Belt of Detroit and, to a similar degree, the industrial wastelands of the Midlands and the North of England, the 'post-industrial' a euphemism for the elision of jobs in primary and secondary industries in Birmingham, Stoke-on-Trent, Manchester, Sheffield and Liverpool. Embracing automation in its car plants, the auto industry removed the human body from the production line and replaced it with the rhythmic robot, the technological habitus organised into limbs without bodies. These tireless, 24/7 workers operated in the dark, and, in common with arcade videogames, were made in Japan and deployed in America and the UK.

Detroit is the city of the future. Its recent bankruptcy and lack of commitment to the social contract of education of its young and the provision of universal public services (e.g. mains water) pushes it beyond capitalism: it is so hollowed out by the machines of the future that capital itself, that human invention *par excellence*, has escaped, leaving a sci-artifice of murals and museums, statues and streets. Before this, in 1987, whilst still in the throes of the shift to the jobless post-industrial, Paul Verhoeven's *RoboCop* presented the Motor City as the bodiless posthuman, the melding of Catholic police officer Alex Murphy with the techno-capital provided by Omni Consumer Products (OCP) to generate an indestructible sheen of law enforcement. Murphy, although legally dead, is provided the opportunity to live on in a shell of metal and glossia of voice-synthesis, biology sustained through liquid food, machine maintained via mains electricity. RoboCop exists only to serve the code, both computer and legislative. Consumption is ancillary and used only to sustain the body that permits ethical decisions to be made, which are dictated not by the social contract of a democratic society, but by the profit motive of OCP. RoboCop's three primary directives appear as a utopian adaptation of Asimov's three laws of the robot, but a fourth directive hidden deep in the code prohibits RoboCop from arresting any employee of OCP.

RoboCop shifts the responsibility of the rule of law on to the machine, which resembles, both figuratively and physically, the individual and collective human, but takes these to their omega point. At the individual level, RoboCop is a 'uniform', in terms of being part of the corpus of police and a uniform cyborg in a city reliant on robots for production. At the collective level, RoboCop symbolises capital accelerated to its outer limits. Crime syndicates, operating under the umbrella of OCP, run black markets in drugs and weapons, whose underground profits feed into the corporation's bottom line. Therefore, RoboCop becomes symbolic of the past, before capitalism fled, a walking technological habitus, production line robots animated in a posthuman body. It is also figurative of the future where the body is too vulnerable, too fleshy to survive both the urban jungle and the ethical quandaries which are demanded of it. Only code can make decisions that are unquestioned, whereas the body and mind will always ask what the future holds. Code is of the future, and in knowing what it looks like follows the shortest course towards it. The trick is in navigating the labyrinth grids of capitalism to find the code to push beyond the final level.

6

Grids and Guidebooks: Beyond the Code

Pac-Manhattan is a 2004 game developed by New York University's Interactive Telecommunications program. While its debut in the early years of the 21st century demonstrates *Pac-Man*'s longevity, it is a simultaneous testament to the transmediality of the 1980 original. The game mechanics of *Pac-Manhattan* remain the same. Four ghosts take on a singular Pac-Man, except this is set on the streets of New York rather than an arcade machine. As the game moves from its native environment of the arcade and takes to the streets of New York it is no longer tactically pure. Neither the ghosts nor Pac-Man have access to all of the information at any given time, but instead communicate via mobile phones and are garnered with eyes-on target support by coordinators in a control room who are able to approximate the location of Pac-Man on a grid-like representation of Washington Square Park in Manhattan.

The genesis of *Pac-Manhattan* appears as a reversal of the creation of the original arcade game. Chris Hall co-creator of *Pac-Manhattan* recalls the inception for the game, 'One afternoon we were looking at a map of the campus area of New York University and noticed that Washington Square Park really maps well to the ghost pen of the original *Pac-Man*.'[1] This reveals an important digression in the development of the game from Iwatani's beginnings which were sited on the universals of survival and eating through to Hall's interpretation which are based on the abstraction of urban space. Whereas Iwatani, for technical, cultural and aesthetic reasons, started with symbols, Hall looked to the representation of space, firstly in the game (the 'ghost pen') and then how the space of Washington Square Park was abstracted on to the grids and contours of a map, before being re-represented at an urban level – itself organised in the gridiron structure common to American cities – and then through the surveillance technology in the control room, which enables the ghosts to chase Pac-Man and defeat him – which they *always* do.

As seen throughout this book, the synonymous geometric shapes of the grid, the maze, the labyrinth or the court are central to the representation of space in capitalism. These representations are used in different ways, but in any iteration they serve the accumulation of capital. Supermarkets are organised in a structure which at once provides relatively simple navigation given that the shortest distance between two points is always a straight line, whilst simultaneously making the most simple items of our daily bread and milk the most difficult items to attain given they are located diagonally as far as possible from the entrance. Meanwhile, convenience stores, although mapped in a similar grid-like structure, ask the punter to pay a cash premium for providing easy access to the high energy, high risk commodities of alcohol, chocolate, tobacco and lottery tickets. Convenience comes at a cost. Ceasing circulation in the supermarket will almost certainly end with validation as to the abstract position of the customer in the supermarket chain. Loyalty cards are swiped, served by a code to provide personalised possibilities of future consumption. The use of self-service checkouts, latter day fruit machines with screens and slots for money, is itself a grid of responses, the human twitching in response to the machinic stimulation proffered by numeric keypads and automated weighing of goods.

Grid-like structures in their many manifestations have been used throughout history, their abstract spaces providing a notion of the organisation knowledge, as with agrarian fields and rice paddies, but also providing a space for the unknown, as seen with labyrinths and mazes. Contemporary philosophers identify with the grid as one of the pre-eminent forms of capitalism: for

Guy Debord it is 'revealed as the true figure of capitalism'.[2] It appears everywhere in everyday life, in the domestic realm of drain networks and their covers, brickwork, rooftops, the public spaces of streets and subway systems, the digital spaces of going 'off' or 'on' the grid of the Internet, the silicon circuit boards which drive it, through to the leisure of board games in chess and *Monopoly*.[3] For Henri Lefebvre, these geometric forms are introduced via the employment of technology in the everyday as 'technology introduces a new form into a pre-existing space – generally a rectilinear or rectangular form such as meshwork or chequerwork'.[4] In common with much, perhaps even all, of the capitalist system, from the market square to the welfare state, these are forms and entities which have been *appropriated* by the system.

Money and markets are not in and of themselves capital, they are utilised by capital towards its own ends. Marketplaces in the centre of towns and cities throughout the world have always been arenas where commerce meets culture: the grid-like maze of streets surrounding Krakow lead to the Gothic square which is an ancient centre of trade. The cloth markets which are permanently located there buy and sell amber and linen; the similarity of their offerings both keep costs to the customer down and allow for relationships based on barter and bargaining to be initiated. The National Health Service, a public good which rightfully resists marketisation of its own services, has taken advantage of its position as the largest single buyer of pharmaceuticals in Europe to keep its own purchasing costs down. Competition impels innovation in prescription drugs and street drugs alike: the more powerful the strain of the disease, the more powerful the strain of genetically modified plants to mitigate the pain.

Like money and markets, capitalism is a human invention. In fact, capital has become like *Pac-Man* in its avaricious and voracious consumption of natural resources, its predilection for chewing up human labour and spitting it out to return, ghostlike, exhausted and spent, to the living room or hotbed at the end of the day. Even play itself mimics the system, pay-to-play mechanics are based around the acquisition of individual skills to live, thrive and survive in the system, with the evolution of this, 'pay-to-win', meaning that the greater the capital acquisition, the more extended the play: better education, better healthcare, better opportunities, more credit. The 'system' itself is excused in this because it is said to be *human nature* that leads us to this point. It is widely understood that humans, through some Pac-Man principle of being hooked into the state of nature, not only want more than the person next to us, but also want to be able to show and tell everyone about it, hence the popularity of social media. Yet, as seen in chapter three it is the human spirit that counters the very exigencies of capitalism and in chapter five it is human inquisition and innovation which takes the body and mind beyond capitalism, returning from a possible future which is post-capitalist precisely because it is post-human. The key here, like the Pac-player guiding Pac-Man through the labyrinth structures of the maze, is to navigate the *human* through the grid, which, although often seen as the pre-eminent form of capitalism, is merely a representation of it. As the guidebooks published around *Pac-Man* in the early 1980s demonstrate, it is the unknown ends which drive the human race towards new beginnings. The unknown provides something which at first appears impossible, but then becomes achievable through dint of a change in perception, approach or attitude. This chapter will examine the possibility inherent in the drive inquisition and innovation and what happens at the end of the game.

Writing in 1974 French philosopher Henri Lefebvre offers a way to critique the capitalist form of the grid: 'the concept of the grid, like the concepts of the model and the code is itself not above reproach... all such concepts have a precise aim, which is to eliminate contradictions, to demonstrate a coherence'.[4]

As seen throughout this book, the Pac-Man principle adheres to the idea that challenges to the pressures and constraints of capitalism come from within. Capitalism, with its predilection for reversibility evidenced in its provision of the welfare/warfare speed/inertia upgrade/obsolescence contradictions, is critical enough of its own position as a system constantly on the brink of crisis and implosion. This is a historical position and various critiques see the capitalist system itself as the best method for escaping these inherent instabilities. As Lefebvre observes, capitalism's own desired end point appears to be the one thing that it can never achieve: the stability and uniformity offered by a grid-like structure. Production lines of robots and the organisation of space from streets to supermarkets attest to this desire, yet capitalism returns like a ghost from one death to the next, desperately lurking in the shadows for the next area to appropriate. For many on the left, including the UK Labour party, this eventual stability can only be found in traditional 'Marxist' positions when neither contemporary economic nor social conditions lend themselves to this approach. Nevertheless, the principle remains the same in that the resolution lies within the system.

This is especially the case when the principle – and therefore the escape route itself – appears as an impossibility. *Pac-Man*'s own position within this structure as one of the enduring symbols on the techno-leisure-capital continuum attests to this. In his assessment of the intricacies of the game, media scholar James Newman chimes with Lefebvre's own assessment of the grid when referring to *Pac-Man*'s maze which is 'constant and consistent across the entire game... [it] has the duality in being the route in and out of danger'.[5] This is entirely cogent with Debord's reading of the grid in his film, *In girum imus nocte et consumimur igni* (1978), which, as Noys identifies, 'stresses the tension built into the grid'.[6] Again, the contradictions that lie at the heart of the capitalist project are apparent in its forms as well as its processes. Movement through the grid, as with much of capitalism, cannot be achieved without being defined in relation to something else, often its dialectical opposite, in this case being the simultaneous source of danger and its escape route. At the same time this raises a further challenge. There is no exit from this grid for Pac-Man, or the player. This is the hell of the same. The famous 'wraparound avenues', which are presented as an escape route, bring Pac-Man, portal-like, back to the other side of the grid. Even the chomping of the final pill, symbol or dot on a level re-emphasises the repetition of capitalism which is concurrently able to possess the past as well as populate the future. As in the labyrinth of antiquity so in posthuman production lines, where, as Borges attests, 'one of the free sides leads to a narrow hallway which opens up onto a gallery identical to the first and all the rest'.[7]

Early guidebooks hint at the infinity of the code of *Pac-Man*. Like many games of the time, this was a game deemed to be so difficult that the end point would never be reached, or, if it were to happen, then the machine would turn over and reset. This happens to the recording of the score: as the counter ticks over a million points, the record returns to zero and play continues. This is a process, which, according to Noys, Debord is acutely aware of. Whilst time is calcified in space, as with the infinite replication of the grid and the code that drives it, the *effects* of time cannot be so easily rebuffed. Proficiency and expertise on the side of the player who turns over the machine is a clear signal that while space can be represented and re-represented over and over, it is not so straightforward to manipulate time. Debord also views the spatial and architectural constraints of the grid as blocking the revolutionary element of play, a quality evinced in Mihaly Csíkszentmihalyi's famous account of 'flow' where an individual is so immersed in a task that they lose track of time.[8] This happens in tasks as variant as running, rock-climbing, software programming, knitting and playing videogames.

So, while the tensions of the grid are not always evident in space, which replicates from one iteration to the next, they are embedded in the passage of time. The score, clocking up and ticking over is witness to this: the grid stays the same, but the recording of it alters through, with and over time. The same inconsistency can be seen in the recording of events themselves within the game, which both attest to the unevenness of the unknown and the problem of relying on spatial formations alone for the development of economic and social models. Even as the grid of capital aims for innate stability, the unknown promotes conjecture and leads to unreliable recording of the passage of time, or history, as it is commonly known.

An early guide to *Pac-Man* observes that when a game is extended through proficiency of the player, the manufacturer subsequently introduced 'a rash of fiendish new programs designed to shorten playing time'[9] including speeding the game up, introducing new artificial intelligence (AI) routines and even stripping the ghosts of their AI routine completely to make them move randomly. Further investigation revealed that while there were indeed 'fast' and 'slow' versions of the game which were designed to shorten time at the machine, the 'randomisation' of ghosts was a myth, showing that in all falsehood it is kernel of truth which ensures some authenticity. These aberrations, in the manufacturer's attempts to manipulate the game, in the player's utilisation and experience of time and the consequent recording of it, begin to reveal the chink in the code that will allow the Pac-player to move beyond abstract notions of space and into a related, but highly personal, temporal experience.

Ken Uston wrote a 1982 standalone guide to the game, *Mastering Pac-Man*. As a professional gambler, a teacher of blackjack and writer of several books on applying logic to chance, his use of charts and strategies to navigate the grids and code of *Pac-Man* is an illustration of the natural predilection for rational behaviour and efficiency that made him a millionaire, achieved through the gaming and playing of the tables and using the rules and processes of the game to his advantage. A similar line is invoked in his book, as Uston breaks down the game into sequences which can be learnt and applied to the game to maximise player score. Uston, ever seeking the profit motive, even encourages gamers to hustle on games, where stakes on Las Vegas Pac-machines reached between $50–$100. A postcard from the fringes of casino capitalism, Uston nevertheless remained convinced of the infinity of the code of *Pac-Man*, believing that the game would go on forever and the only way to 'beat' the game was to walk away from it. Akin to withdrawing to the woods to live in a log cabin and live off the land, the casino capitalist admits that you 'might walk away from the machine in midgame out of sheer boredom or fatigue'.[10]

The idea or feeling of ennui setting in is common to any parent who has experienced the slight existential death of waiting at ballet class for their children, a piecemeal worker on a production line sticking pieces of foam together with noxious adhesives and the agency staffer enduring another office team meeting which masquerades as work. Even in the excitement of setting high scores, of gambling, of witnessing the pre-eminent economic, social and political model of our time implode before our very eyes, we still return to the principle of boredom. This is because, in common with Uston and, as Carl Cederstrom and Peter Fleming bitterly highlight, 'capitalism exists only for itself. It has become its own final destination'.[11] It seems as though there is no alternative to capitalist realism, that, unlike for 1990s ravers, the last true counterculture of contemporary society, there is no exit, no future. Like Pac-Man we may look for a way out, but just find ourselves popping up on the other side of the grid, looking at the same space from a different angle in an endless cycle of code and consumption.

If the answer does come from within, from the reversibility that is inherent in the capitalist project, then it is not only the forms, but capitalism's processes and attitudes that must be employed to move beyond capitalism. If Max Weber sees the ultimate representation of the grid in the iron cage of bureaucracy, then employ the Protestant work ethic to attain the spirit of capitalism. However, instead of turning into a ghost, this resolute application will reveal something beyond the code, not at the fringes of casino capitalism, but somewhere beyond it. If Uston is suggesting that capital has no limits, that all that can be done is to walk away from it or vacantly engage with it, then Debord's concept of play, of moving to the limits of capital, to stress the tension in the grid, becomes yet more vital. Indeed, as Noys notes play *is* central to moving to these limits, there is a requirement for 'new forms of play, that do not operate in the circularity of capitalist accumulation'.[12] Taking the essence of capital and play to their logical conclusion, the Pac-Man principle impels the gamer to work hard to play hard.

The perfect place for this to happen is in the code-riven, consumer-driven societies of the West. Anglo-Saxon culture and language, often derided for its association with the excesses of capital, importantly also has different words for 'play' and 'game'. More vitally, the use of the verb 'play' has several meanings alongside playing a game. It is suggestive of tension in the grid: if a component has 'play' in it, it is under stress and, moving around, it is liable to break; a tooth with 'play' is on the verge of falling out. It is play that pushes at the limit of capital, but working hard at play is a serious – and labour intensive – business. Uston himself hints at the possibilities inherent in this playful application earlier in his book, intimating that if the recommended rational paths are followed then the 'sky is the literally the limit for the player'[13] in terms of score.

Jim Sykora and John Birkner's guidebook of the same year, *The Video Master's Guide to Pac-Man*, provides the breakthrough that had been intimated by critics of the grid and the authors of guides to *Pac-Man*. Following a line of sequential learning through patterns similar to Uston, the cover of the book claims to be able to teach the player to: 'Beat the program, see it end!' This is not an empty promise. An affidavit on the final page assures the reader that John Birkner could 'baffle a machine so much that it gave up and broke down'[14] and then, on pages 62 and 63, there is an illustration of level 256 where part of the grid breaks down into code which makes it impossible for the Pac-player to navigate through and beyond. Appositely, the authors note that the machine is 'not without its limits... the board divides in half and the monsters begin attacking from unpredictable locations. Mass confusion occurs and the game cannot continue. A player who achieves this level has technically beaten the computer'.[15]

What is key here is that there *are* limits to the grid, manifested in the mathematical calculations, the code, that drives the game. The human Pac-player has pushed the grid to the limit and finds in that codified representation of space, the grid breaks down into little more than nonsense. For a game that was never meant to end, that should be infinite in its spaces and repetition, this is a revelation. Level 256 of *Pac-Man*, commonly known as the 'killscreen' or 'split screen', signals the endgame. For some commentators, this shows that there is no joy to be had from the game as there is 'no final victory waiting for Pac-Man, only an empty half-maze full of ghosts'.[16]

Yet this assessment, appealing to the competitive Pac-player who cannot achieve a high score, but only a maximum score, does not appeal to the foundation of the Pac-Man principle. *Pac-Man*, originating from a symbolic culture where meaning was not generated through the saturation of the sign, but instead left to individual interpretation, bridged ideas and challenged conventional understanding in both the East and the West. Was this pizza or *kuchi*? Is this a game about need or greed? Autonomy or control? Surveillance or speed? Capital accumulation or conquest of capital?

The grid revealed on the killscreen reverts back to these

symbols. In Borges' words it has devolved to the pre-modern version of the grid as a 'labyrinth of symbols'.[17] The Pac-player has pushed play to the limits and discovered that capital's pre-emptive spatial formation, based upon the code that drives the information society, the nodes and networks, of which everyone, machine, animal, vegetable, mineral, human is a part, has devolved into its original, interpretative form. This is the end of capital. The Pac-player, in taking the symbol of *Kuchi* to the end, reveals a state where space itself breaks up, breaks down, and there is no exit from. The hypermodern grid has a slight return to its antique origins, but reveals the impossibility of code becoming fully pervasive. This is not a bleak ending, but triumph and testament to the immitigability of the human spirit over the spirit of capitalism. Indeed, on this final level, it is possible to trap the ghosts and leave them to infinitely bob up and down, mimicking Pac-Man without a player, but leaving the Pac-player to explore this now defunct grid, this labyrinth of symbols, with true knowledge of the unknown: there remains no known way beyond this point (without manipulating the machine outside of its rule-sets). Is transcendence in knowing the unknown? Is true faith a belief in the unseen? At this endgame, beyond the code, beyond the limits of capital there are symbols and the infinite interpretation familiar to those who do not only see space as a means of representation, but time as a flow of perception.

Noys, writing of Debord, identifies the ultimate revolutionary element as water. Fire consumes itself, leaving a scorched Earth behind. It is at once there, then, like a capitalist worker, burnt out. Spent. Water flows through space, making its own gullies, rivulets and ravines. It is through water that the passage of time leads to the formation of space, of grand fjords from glaciers, of islands of reflection. Patiently, often changing form, it opens new channels of communication, its rhythms incessant, sometimes ruinous, sometimes placatory.

In the present day, the great contemporary Pac-Man players

play not for the highest score, but for the lowest time to attain the maximum score. The flow of play, when fully invested in activity, becomes not about the formation of space, or its eventual dissolving into sign systems and symbols, but about the time needed to reach that point. Water, like play, flows towards its end, showing the past, illuminating the present, heralding the future. The Pac-Man principle shows what that future can be like when it is carefully cultivated time-as-process which is the aim, not the pursuit of space-as-ends. As a product of capital, code shows the limits of space. Pushing beyond the code, the human spirit shows the possibilities of time.

7

Afterword by Toru Iwatani

Video games are unusual products that differ from other industrial goods in which electrical power, machines, and creative work are integrated. They are an aggregation of a variety of academic disciplines, including engineering, literature, the arts, and psychology, and can be considered a cultural tool for the 'fun' required by society.

The common feature shared by all these games that become audience hits is the sensitive attention paid by creators to player shifts in mood. Most players appear to be playing games according to a set of rules, but they are actually playing with the mind of the creator. It's important for the creator to think in terms of the player's feelings and not only be service-minded but also be considerate of the player. I believe a good game is a product of something that both the creator and player will find worthwhile.

The game arcades in late 1970s were the places for boys to play rather rough 'kill the alien' type of games. So I wanted to turn it into a brighter and more fun place where women and couples could feel comfortable going. So I designed a game for women with a focus on the concept of 'eating'. I aimed to create a fun and cute game that can be played easily with simple control. The idea of a power pellet that changes PAC-MAN and the ghosts' situation is similar to the spinach from the TV animation Popeye and the relationship between PAC-MAN and ghosts is influenced by Tom and Jerry who are quasi-enemies.

When I was conceptualizing the game with the keyword 'eat', I ordered a pizza for lunch and took a slice. When I saw the remaining shape, I immediately thought, 'This is it!' and it lead me to the idea of what we now know as PAC-MAN.

Both PACMAN and ghosts are designed simple and cute, and appealing to everyone including women.

Game elements of PAC-MAN

1. Simple game rules and easily understandable goals. The goal of the game is to eat all of the pellets inside a maze, avoiding the four ghosts through controlling the protagonist PAC-MAN. When you see the screen, you would immediately realize what to do even before playing.
2. Sense of design and character. The design of PAC-MAN is simple, and the design of colorful ghosts is enemy role, but ghosts are cute and likable. The designs of both imbue the avatars with character.
3. Simple controls. You can only move PAC-MAN in four directions: up, down, left, and right.

Further: As university research

I left the video game industry to work at a university and to pursue the study of Game Theory for social good, meaning, the role of games, based on my experience and knowledge in creating games for 30 years. Currently, I am teaching students Game Theory, Game Planning, and Serious Games in the Department of Game, Faculty of Arts at Tokyo Polytechnic University. Truly, thank you very much.

Toru Iwatani
Tokyo
May 2017

Endnotes

In Defence of *Pac-Man*

1. Henry Jenkins. *Convergence Culture: Where Old and New Media Collide* (New York: New York University Press, 2007)
2. Susan Lammers. 'Toru Iwatani, 1986 PacMan Designer.' *Programmers at Work*, available at https://programmersatwork. wordpress.com/toru-iwatani-1986-pacman-designer/ – accessed 20th July 2016
3. Lammers. 'Toru Iwatani, 1986 PacMan Designer' available at https://programmersatwork.wordpress.com/toru-iwatani-1986-pacman-designer/
4. Martin Amis. *Invasion of the Space Invaders* (London: Hutchinson, 1982), page 57
5. Lammers. 'Toru Iwatani, 1986 PacMan Designer' available at https://programmersatwork.wordpress.com/toru-iwatani-1986-pacman-designer/
6. Carl Cederstrom and Peter Fleming. *Dead Man Working* (Alresford: Zero Books, 2012)
7. Carly A. Kocurek. 'Coin-Drop Capitalism' in *Before the Crash: Early Video Game History*, Mark JP Wolf, Editor (Detroit: Wayne State University Press, 2004), page 204
8. David Harvey. *The Condition of Postmodernity* (Oxford: Blackwell, 1991)
9. Martin Amis. *Invasion of the Space Invaders* (London: Hutchinson, 1982), page 57
10. Jean Baudrillard. *The Transparency of Evil* (London: Verso, 1993), page 62

Speed and Space: The Places and Times of *Pac-Man*

1. See Raiford Guins' '"Intruder Alert! Intruder Alert!" Video Games in Space.' *Journal of Visual Culture*, 3(2), 2004, pages 195–211

2. Anna McCarthy. *Ambient Television: Visual Culture and Public Space* (Durham, North Carolina: Duke University Press, 2001)

3. Martin Amis. *Invasion of the Space Invaders* (London: Hutchinson, 1982), page 56

4. Jorge Luis Borges. *Labyrinths* (London: Penguin, 2000)

5. Al Alcorn. 'When Arcades Ruled the World: The Genesis of an Industry.' *Retro Gamer*, Issue 127, April 2014

6. Paul Virilio. *Negative Horizon* (London: Continuum, 2008), page 110

7. Martin Amis. *Invasion of the Space Invaders* (London: Hutchinson, 1982), page 57

Ghostware: The Hauntologies of *Pac-Man*

1. Jeremy Bentham. *Panopticon; Or, the Inspection-House* (Gloucester: Dodo Press, 2008)

2. Thomas Mathiesen. 'The Viewer Society'. *Theoretical Criminology*, Vol 1(2), Sage Publications, London (1997)

3. Lev Manovich. 'Film/Telecommunication – Benjamin/Virilio' available at http://faculty.dwc.edu/wellman/Vir-Benj.htm – accessed 7th October 2016

4. Grègoire Chamayou. *Drone Theory* (London: Penguin, 2015)

5. Jamey Pittman. 'The Pac-Man Dossier' available at http://www.gamasutra.com/view/feature/3938/the_pacman_dossier.php?print=1 – accessed 7th October 2016

6. Jamey Pittman. 'The Pac-Man Dossier' available at http://www.gamasutra.com/view/feature/3938/the_pacman_dossier.php?print=1 – accessed 7th October 2016. As a side note, *'oitsuke, oikose'*, meaning 'catch-up, overtake', was employed by Japan as a credible economic policy in its competition with the West in the 19th century. See Chris Rowthorn, *Lonely Planet: Japan* (Victoria: Lonely Planet), page 807 for further discussion.

7. There are a range of other theories including that Elroy

relates to the Celtic moniker of 'red haired youth', befitting of the colour of Blinky and the link between Elroy, the youngest member of *The Jetsons* TV show which was popular throughout the 1980s. See http://www.classicarcadegaming. com/forums/index.php?topic=3214.0 for further discussion.

8. Elizabeth and Geoffrey Loftus. *Mind at Play: The Psychology of Video Games* (New York: Basic Books, 1983)

9. Thorstein Veblen. *The Theory of the Leisure Class* (Oxford: Oxford University Press, 2009)

10. Benjamin Noys. *Malign Velocities: Accelerationism and Capitalism* (Alresford: Zero Books, 2014), page 99

11. Jamey Pittman. 'The Pac-Man Dossier' available at http:// www.gamasutra.com/view/feature/3938/the_pacman_ dossier.php?print=1 – accessed 7th October 2016

12. Sun Tzu. *The Art of War* (Boston, Massachusetts: Shambhala Publications, 1988)

13. Umberto Eco. *The Name of the Rose* (London: Vintage, 2004)

14. Grègoire Chamayou. *Drone Theory* (London: Penguin, 2015), page 78

15. Grègoire Chamayou. *Drone Theory* (London: Penguin, 2015), page 117

16. Grègoire Chamayou. *Drone Theory* (London: Penguin, 2015), page 84

17. Bernard Stiegler. 'The Disaffected Individual in the Process of Psychic and Collective Disindividuation' available at http://www.arsindustrialis.org/disaffected-individual- process-psychic-and-collective-disindividuation – accessed 21st December 2016

18. Grègoire Chamayou. *Drone Theory* (London: Penguin, 2015), page 120

19. Jamey Pittman. 'The Pac-Man Dossier' available at http:// www.gamasutra.com/view/feature/3938/the_pacman_ dossier.php?print=1 – accessed 21st December 2016

The Politics of Pac-Land

1. Paul Virilio. *Negative Horizon* (London: Continuum, 2008), page 97
2. Gerry Coulter. 'Baudrillard on Terrorism and War in Times of Hyper-mobility'. *International Journal of Safety and Security in Tourism/Hospitality*, Volume 13, Number 1, 2015, available at http://www.palermo.edu/Archivos_content/2015/econo micas/journal-tourism/edicion13/03_Baudrillard_on_ Terrorism_and_War.pdf – accessed 14th March 2017
3. Zygmunt Bauman. *Consuming Life* (Cambridge: Polity, 2007), page 98
4. Herbert Marcuse. *One-Dimensional Man* (Abingdon: Routledge, 2007), page 96
5. Herbert Marcuse. *One-Dimensional Man* (Abingdon: Routledge, 2007), page 14
6. Jean Baudrillard. *Symbolic Exchange and Death* (London: Sage, 1993), page 62
7. Jean Baudrillard. *Symbolic Exchange and Death* (London: Sage, 1993), page 62
8. Zygmunt Bauman. 'Inhumanity Is Part of Human Nature: Part II' available at http://salon.eu.sk/en/archiv/1143 – accessed 13th March 2017
9. Zygmunt Bauman. 'Inhumanity Is Part of Human Nature: Part II' available at http://salon.eu.sk/en/archiv/1143 – accessed 13th March 2017
10. Jean Baudrillard. *Symbolic Exchange and Death* (London: Sage, 1993), page 63
11. Jean Baudrillard. *The Spirit of Terrorism* (London: Verso, 2002), page 23
12. Jean Baudrillard. *The Spirit of Terrorism* (London: Verso, 2002), page 23

Accelerate Your Mind: The Soundscapes of *Pac-Man*

1. Mark JP Wolf. 'Abstraction in the Videogame' in *The Video*

Game Theory Reader (Abingdon: Routledge, 2003), page 47

2. Steven L. Kent. *The First Quarter: A 25-Year History of Video Games* (Bothell: BWD Press, 2000)

3. Marshall McLuhan. *Understanding Media: The Extensions of Man* (London: Routledge, 2001), page 258

4. Peter Freund. 'Civilised Bodies Redux: Seams in the Cyborg', *Social Theory and Health* 2(3): 273–289, page 273 (2004)

5. Peter Freund. 'Civilised Bodies Redux: Seams in the Cyborg', *Social Theory and Health* 2(3): 273–289, page 282 (2004)

6. Karen Collins. 'Loops and bloops: music of the Commodore 64 games'. *Soundscapes* 8 (2006) available at: http://www.icce.rug.nl/~soundscapes/VOLUME08/Loops_and_bloops.shtml – accessed 3rd February 2017

7. Gary Western. 'Top Score: The Evolution and Significance of Video Game Music' presentation given at CSU Monterey Bay, February 26th 2011, available at: https://garywestern.files.wordpress.com/2011/04/garywestern_topscore.pdf – accessed 3rd February 2017

8. Marcus Brigstocke. 'Pac-Man' available at: https://web.archive.org/web/20120516182307/http://www.marcusbrigstocke.com/pacman.php – accessed 30th March 2017

9. Benjamin Noys. 'Days of Phuture Past: Accelerationism in the Present Moment' presentation given at 'Accelerationism: A Symposium on Tendencies in Capitalism', Berlin, 14th December 2013, page 5

10. Benjamin Noys. 'Days of Phuture Past: Accelerationism in the Present Moment' presentation given at 'Accelerationism: A Symposium on Tendencies in Capitalism', Berlin, 14th December 2013, page 5

11. Alex Wade. *Playback: A Genealogy of 1980s British Videogames* (New York: Bloomsbury, 2016), pages 51–76

12. John O'Connell. 'Interview with Richard D. James'. *The Face*, October 2001, available at https://web.archive.org/web/20080615033834/http://www.aphextwin.nu/

learn/100771194880071.shtml – accessed 7th February 2017

13. Benjamin Noys. 'Dance and Die: Obsolescence and Embedded Aesthetics of Acceleration' available at https://www.academia.edu/6129466/Dance_and_Die – accessed 30th March 2017, page 4

14. Benjamin Noys. 'Dance and Die: Obsolescence and Embedded Aesthetics of Acceleration' available at https://www.academia.edu/6129466/Dance_and_Die – accessed 30th March 2017, page 4

Grids and Guidebooks: Beyond the Code

1. Chris Hall. 'Urban Game'. *Current TV*, available at: http://www.pacmanhattan.com/videos.php (2004)

2. Benjamin Noys. 'Guy Debord's Time-Image: *In girum imus nocte et consumimur igni* (1978)'. *Grey Room* 52, 94–107, page 99 (2013)

3. Benjamin Noys. 'Guy Debord's Time-Image: *In girum imus nocte et consumimur igni* (1978)'. *Grey Room* 52, 94–107, page 99 (2013)

4. Henri Lefebvre. *The Production of Space* (Oxford: Blackwell, 2004), page 165

5. James Newman. 'Mazes, monsters and multicursality. Mastering Pac-Man 1980–2016'. *Cogent Arts and Humanities* 3 (2016), page 5

6. Benjamin Noys. 'Guy Debord's Time-Image: *In girum imus nocte et consumimur igni* (1978)'. *Grey Room* 52, 94–107, page 99 (2013)

7. Jorge Luis Borges. *Labyrinths* (London: Penguin, 2000), page 78

8. Mihaly Csíkszentmihalyi. 'The flow experience and its significance for human psychology' in *Optimal Experience: Psychological Studies of Flow in Consciousness* (Cambridge: Cambridge University Press, 1988), page 15

9. Tom Hirschfield. *How to Master the Video Games* (New York:

Bantam, 1981), page 113

10. Ken Uston. *Mastering Pac-Man* (New York: Signet, 1982), page 124

11. Carl Cederstrom and Peter Fleming. *Dead Man Working* (Abingdon: Zero Books, 2012), page 5

12. Benjamin Noys. 'Guy Debord's Time-Image: *In girum imus nocte et consumimur igni* (1978)'. *Grey Room* 52, 94–107, page 99 (2013)

13. Ken Uston. *Mastering Pac-Man* (New York: Signet, 1982), page 10

14. Jim Sykora and John Birkner. *The Video Master's Guide to Pac-Man* (New York: Bantam Books, 1982), page 84

15. Jim Sykora and John Birkner. *The Video Master's Guide to Pac-Man* (New York: Bantam Books, 1982), page 63

16. Jamey Pittman. 'The Pac-Man Dossier' available at http://www.gamasutra.com/view/feature/3938/the_pacman_dossier.php?print=1 – accessed 24th February 2017

17. Jorge Luis Borges. *Labyrinths* (London: Penguin, 2000), page 84

Zero Books

CULTURE, SOCIETY & POLITICS

Contemporary culture has eliminated the concept and public figure of the intellectual. A cretinous anti-intellectualism presides, cheer-led by hacks in the pay of multinational corporations who reassure their bored readers that there is no need to rouse themselves from their stupor. Zer0 Books knows that another kind of discourse – intellectual without being academic, popular without being populist – is not only possible: it is already flourishing. Zer0 is convinced that in the unthinking, blandly consensual culture in which we live, critical and engaged theoretical reflection is more important than ever before.

If you have enjoyed this book, why not tell other readers by posting a review on your preferred book site.

Recent bestsellers from Zero Books are:

In the Dust of This Planet
Horror of Philosophy vol. 1
Eugene Thacker
In the first of a series of three books on the Horror of
Philosophy, *In the Dust of This Planet* offers the genre of horror
as a way of thinking about the unthinkable.
Paperback: 978-1-84694-676-9 ebook: 978-1-78099-010-1

Capitalist Realism
Is there no alternative?
Mark Fisher
An analysis of the ways in which capitalism has presented itself
as the only realistic political-economic system.
Paperback: 978-1-84694-317-1 ebook: 978-1-78099-734-6

Rebel Rebel
Chris O'Leary
David Bowie: every single song. Everything you want to know,
everything you didn't know.
Paperback: 978-1-78099-244-0 ebook: 978-1-78099-713-1

Cartographies of the Absolute
Alberto Toscano, Jeff Kinkle
An aesthetics of the economy for the twenty-first century.
Paperback: 978-1-78099-275-4 ebook: 978-1-78279-973-3

Malign Velocities

Accelerationism and Capitalism

Benjamin Noys

Longlisted for the Bread and Roses Prize 2015, *Malign Velocities* argues against the need for speed, tracking acceleration as the symptom of the ongoing crises of capitalism.

Paperback: 978-1-78279-300-7 ebook: 978-1-78279-299-4

Meat Market

Female flesh under Capitalism

Laurie Penny

A feminist dissection of women's bodies as the fleshy fulcrum of capitalist cannibalism, whereby women are both consumers and consumed.

Paperback: 978-1-84694-521-2 ebook: 978-1-84694-782-7

Poor but Sexy

Culture Clashes in Europe East and West

Agata Pyzik

How the East stayed East and the West stayed West.

Paperback: 978-1-78099-394-2 ebook: 978-1-78099-395-9

Romeo and Juliet in Palestine

Teaching Under Occupation

Tom Sperlinger

Life in the West Bank, the nature of pedagogy and the role of a university under occupation.

Paperback: 978-1-78279-637-4 ebook: 978-1-78279-636-7

Sweetening the Pill
or How We Got Hooked on Hormonal Birth Control
Holly Grigg-Spall
Has contraception liberated or oppressed women? *Sweetening the Pill* breaks the silence on the dark side of hormonal contraception.
Paperback: 978-1-78099-607-3 ebook: 978-1-78099-608-0

Why Are We The Good Guys?
Reclaiming Your Mind from the Delusions of Propaganda
David Cromwell
A provocative challenge to the standard ideology that Western power is a benevolent force in the world.
Paperback: 978-1-78099-365-2 ebook: 978-1-78099-366-9

Readers of ebooks can buy or view any of these bestsellers by clicking on the live link in the title. Most titles are published in paperback and as an ebook. Paperbacks are available in traditional bookshops. Both print and ebook formats are available online.

Find more titles and sign up to our readers' newsletter at http://www.johnhuntpublishing.com/culture-and-politics

Follow us on Facebook
at https://www.facebook.com/ZeroBooks

and Twitter at https://twitter.com/Zer0Books